ENGLISH
FOR EVERYONE

PRACTICE BOOK LEVEL ❷

BUSINESS ENGLISH

 FREE AUDIO
website and app
www.dkefe.com

Authors

Thomas Booth worked for 10 years as an English-language teacher in Poland and Russia. He now lives in England, where he works as an editor and English-language materials writer, notably of course books and vocabulary textbooks.

Trish Burrow worked for seven years as a teacher and teacher trainer in Poland and UK summer schools. After a year working in a UK college as an ELT lecturer, she worked as an editor of exams materials and then English-language teaching materials. She lives in the UK and is a freelance writer and editor.

Course consultant

Tim Bowen has taught English and trained teachers in more than 30 countries worldwide. He is the co-author of works on pronunciation teaching and language-teaching methodology, and author of numerous books for English-language teachers. He is currently a freelance materials writer, editor, and translator. He is a member of the Chartered Institute of Linguists.

Language consultant

Professor Susan Barduhn is an experienced English-language teacher, teacher trainer, and author, who has contributed to numerous publications. In addition to directing English-language courses in at least four different continents, she has been President of the International Association of Teachers of English as a Foreign Language, and an adviser to the British Council and the US State Department. She is currently a Professor at the School for International Training in Vermont, USA.

ENGLISH
FOR EVERYONE

PRACTICE BOOK **LEVEL 2**
BUSINESS ENGLISH

Project Editors Lili Bryant, Laura Sandford
Art Editors Chrissy Barnard, Paul Drislane, Michelle Staples
Editor Ben Ffrancon Davies
Editorial Assistants Sarah Edwards, Helen Leech
Illustrators Edwood Burn, Michael Parkin, Gus Scott
Managing Editor Daniel Mills
Managing Art Editor Anna Hall
Audio Recording Manager Christine Stroyan
Jacket Designer Ira Sharma
Jacket Editor Claire Gell
Managing Jacket Editor Saloni Singh
Jacket Design Development Manager Sophia MTT
Producer, Pre-production Andy Hilliard
Producer Mary Slater
Publisher Andrew Macintyre
Art Director Karen Self
Publishing Director Jonathan Metcalf

DK India
Senior Managing Art Editor Arunesh Talapatra
Senior Art Editor Chhaya Sajwan
Art Editors Meenal Goel, Roshni Kapur
Assistant Art Editor Rohit Dev Bhardwaj
Illustrators Manish Bhatt, Arun Pottirayil,
Sachin Tanwar, Mohd Zishan
Editorial Coordinator Priyanka Sharma
Pre-production Manager Balwant Singh
Senior DTP Designers Harish Aggarwal, Vishal Bhatia
DTP Designer Jaypal Chauhan

First published in Great Britain in 2017
by Dorling Kindersley Limited
DK, One Embassy Gardens, 8 Viaduct Gardens,
London, SW11 7BW

The authorised representative in the EEA is
Dorling Kindersley Verlag GmbH. Arnulfstr. 124,
80636 Munich, Germany

A CIP catalogue record for this book
is available from the British Library.
ISBN: 978-0-2412-7515-3

Printed and bound in China

www.dk.com

This book was
made with Forest
Stewardship
Council™ certified
paper – one small
step in DK's
commitment to a
sustainable future.
**Learn more at
www.dk.com/uk/
information/
sustainability**

FSC
www.fsc.org
MIX
Paper | Supporting
responsible forestry
FSC™ C018179

Contents

How the course works   8

01   Introductions   12
New language Present simple and continuous
Vocabulary Etiquette for introductions
New skill Introducing yourself and others

02   Getting to know colleagues   16
New language Past simple and past continuous
Vocabulary Sharing past experiences
New skill Talking about past experiences

03   Vocabulary   20
Departments and roles

04   Talking about changes   22
New language "Used to," "be / get used to"
Vocabulary Small talk
New skill Talking about changes at work

05   Delegating tasks   26
New language Modal verbs for obligation
Vocabulary Delegation and politeness
New skill Delegating tasks to colleagues

06   Vocabulary Money and finance   30

07   Writing a report   32
New language Past perfect and past simple
Vocabulary Formal business English
New skill Writing reports

08 Making apologies 36

New language Present perfect continuous
Vocabulary Apologies
New skill Apologizing on the telephone

09 Vocabulary 40
Communication technology

10 Making plans by email 42

New language Email language
Vocabulary Meetings and workshops
New skill Making plans

11 Keeping clients informed 44

New language Continuous tenses
Vocabulary Arrangements and schedules
New skill Keeping clients informed

12 Informal communication 47

New language Phrasal verbs
Vocabulary Arrangements and plans
New skill Keeping co-workers informed

13 Vocabulary Production 50

14 Describing a process 52

New language The passive voice
Vocabulary Processes and manufacturing
New skill Discussing how things are done

15 Describing a product 56

New language Adjective order
Vocabulary Opinion and fact adjectives
New skill Describing a product

16 Vocabulary 60
Marketing and advertising

17 Marketing a product 62

New language Adjectives and adverbs
Vocabulary Descriptive adjectives
New skill Modifying descriptions of products

18 Advertising and branding 65

New language Intensifiers
Vocabulary "Enough," too," "so," and "such"
New skill Adding emphasis to descriptions

19 Advice and suggestions 68

New language Modal verbs for advice
Vocabulary Workplace pressures
New skill Giving advice

20 Vocabulary 72
Management, leadership, and skills

21 Talking about abilities 74

New language Modal verbs for abilities
Vocabulary Workplace skills
New skill Describing abilities

22 Comparing and contrasting 78
New language Discourse markers
Vocabulary Teamwork and team building
New skill Expressing your ideas

23 Planning events 82
New language Verb patterns
Vocabulary Corporate entertainment
New skill Talking about business events

24 Vocabulary Meetings 86

25 What people said 88
New language Reported speech
Vocabulary Meetings
New skill Reporting what someone said

26 What people asked 92
New language Reported questions
Vocabulary "Have," "make," "get," "do"
New skill Reporting what someone asked

27 Reporting quantities 96
New language "Few," "little," and "all"
Vocabulary Meetings
New skill Talking about quantity

28 Checking information 99
New language Subject questions, question tags
Vocabulary Polite checks and echo questions
New skill Checking information

29 Vocabulary 102
Industries and professional attributes

30 Job descriptions 104
New language Articles
Vocabulary Job descriptions and applications
New skill Describing a job

31 Applying for a job 107
New language Dependent prepositions
Vocabulary Cover-letter vocabulary
New skill Writing a cover letter

32 Job interviews 110
New language Relative clauses
Vocabulary Job interviews
New skill Describing your achievements in detail

33 Vocabulary Business idioms 114

34 Working relationships 116
New language Three-word phrasal verbs
Vocabulary Social media
New skill Social networking

35 Career outcomes 120
New language Modal verbs for possibility
Vocabulary Career development
New skill Talking about the future

36 Vocabulary 124
Office and presentation equipment

37 Structuring a presentation 126
New language Signposting language
Vocabulary Presentation equipment
New skill Structuring a presentation

38 Developing an argument 129
New language Useful presentation language
Vocabulary Presentations
New skill Developing an argument

39 Pitching a product 132
New language Comparatives and superlatives
Vocabulary Product marketing
New skill Comparing products

40 Talking about facts and figures 135
New language Collocations
Vocabulary Business trends
New skill Describing facts and figures

41 Plans and suggestions 138
New language Indirect questions
Vocabulary Business negotiations
New skill Negotiating politely

42 Emphasizing your opinion 142
New language Discourse markers for emphasis
Vocabulary Workplace disagreement
New skill Emphasizing your opinion

43 Discussing conditions 144
New language Conditionals
Vocabulary Negotiating and bargaining
New skill Discussing possibilities

44 Discussing problems 148
New language Third conditional
Vocabulary Workplace mistakes
New skill Talking about past mistakes

Answers 152

How the course works

English for Everyone is designed for people who want to teach themselves the English language. The Business English edition covers essential English phrases and constructions for a wide range of common business scenarios.

Unlike other courses, *English for Everyone* uses images and graphics in all its learning and practice, to help you understand and remember as easily as possible. The best way to learn is to work through the book in order, making full use of the audio available on the website and app. Turn to the practice book at the end of each unit to reinforce your learning with additional exercises.

COURSE BOOK

PRACTICE BOOK

Unit number The book is divided into units. Each practice book unit tests the language taught in the course book unit with the same number.

Practice points Every unit begins with a summary of the key practice points.

Modules Each unit is broken down into modules, which should be done in order. You can take a break from learning after completing any module.

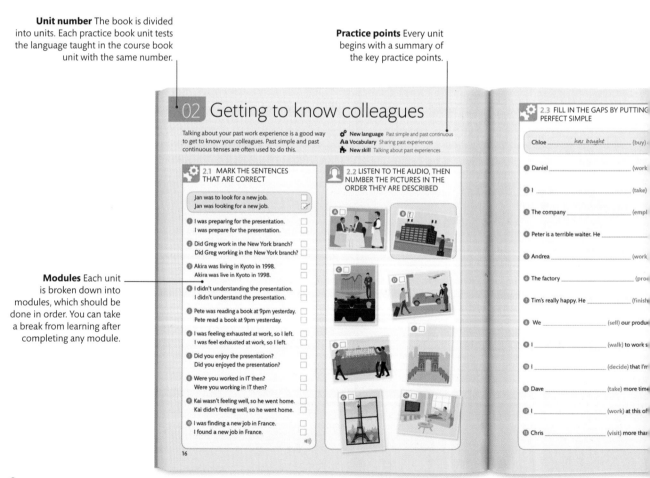

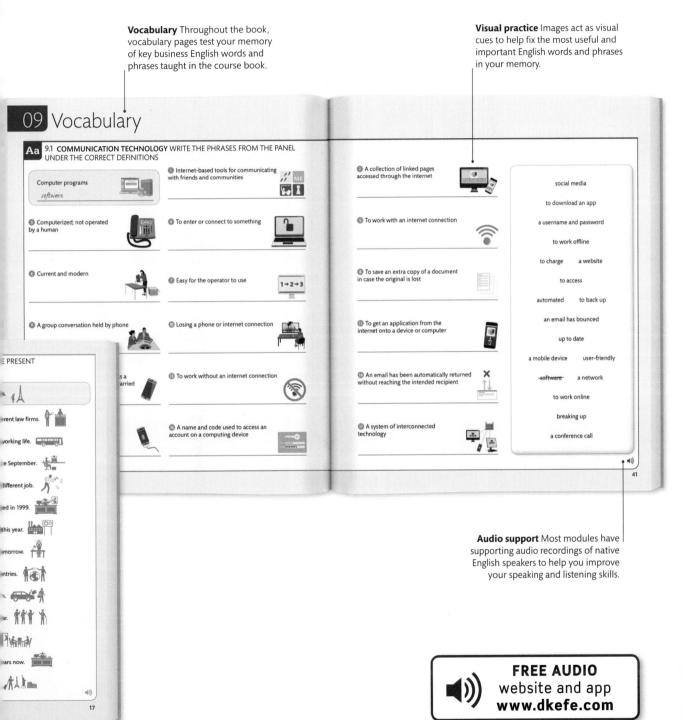

Vocabulary Throughout the book, vocabulary pages test your memory of key business English words and phrases taught in the course book.

Visual practice Images act as visual cues to help fix the most useful and important English words and phrases in your memory.

09 Vocabulary

Aa **9.1 COMMUNICATION TECHNOLOGY** WRITE THE PHRASES FROM THE PANEL UNDER THE CORRECT DEFINITIONS

Computer programs
software

① Internet-based tools for communicating with friends and communities

③ Computerized; not operated by a human

④ To enter or connect to something

⑥ Current and modern

⑦ Easy for the operator to use

⑧ A group conversation held by phone

⑩ Losing a phone or internet connection

⑬ To work without an internet connection

⑭ A name and code used to access an account on a computing device

② A collection of linked pages accessed through the internet

⑤ To work with an internet connection

⑨ To save an extra copy of a document in case the original is lost

⑪ To get an application from the internet onto a device or computer

⑮ An email has been automatically returned without reaching the intended recipient

⑰ A system of interconnected technology

social media

to download an app

a username and password

to work offline

to charge   a website

to access

automated   to back up

an email has bounced

up to date

a mobile device   user-friendly

~~software~~   a network

to work online

breaking up

a conference call

41

Audio support Most modules have supporting audio recordings of native English speakers to help you improve your speaking and listening skills.

FREE AUDIO
website and app
www.dkefe.com

9

Practice modules

Each exercise is carefully graded to drill and test the language taught in the corresponding course book units. Working through the exercises alongside the course book will help you remember what you have learned and become more fluent. Every exercise is introduced with a symbol to indicate which skill is being practiced.

 GRAMMAR
Apply new language rules in different contexts.

 READING
Examine target language in real-life English contexts.

 LISTENING
Test your understanding of spoken English.

 VOCABULARY
Cement your understanding of key vocabulary.

 SPEAKING
Compare your spoken English to model audio recordings.

Module number Every module is identified with a unique number, so you can easily locate answers and related audio.

Exercise instruction Every exercise is introduced with a brief instruction, telling you what you need to do.

Supporting graphics Visual cues are given to help you understand the exercises.

Supporting audio This symbol shows that the answers to the exercise are available as audio tracks. Listen to them after completing the exercise.

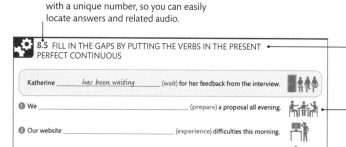

8.5 FILL IN THE GAPS BY PUTTING THE VERBS IN THE PRESENT PERFECT CONTINUOUS

Katherine ___*has been waiting*___ (wait) for her feedback from the interview.

❶ We _____ (prepare) a proposal all evening.

❷ Our website _____ (experience) difficulties this morning.

❸ Chris _____ (work) on that project for three months now.

❹ Our products _____ (not sell) well so far this year.

Space for writing You are encouraged to write your answers in the book for future reference.

Sample answer The first question of each exercise is answered for you, to help make the task easy to understand.

Listening exercise This symbol indicates that you should listen to an audio track in order to answer the questions in the exercise.

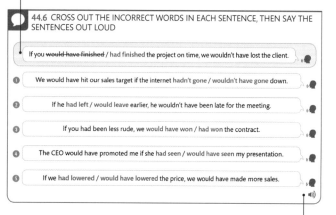

44.6 CROSS OUT THE INCORRECT WORDS IN EACH SENTENCE, THEN SAY THE SENTENCES OUT LOUD

If you ~~would have finished~~ / had finished the project on time, we wouldn't have lost the client.

❶ We would have hit our sales target if the internet hadn't gone / wouldn't have gone down.

❷ If he had left / would leave earlier, he wouldn't have been late for the meeting.

❸ If you had been less rude, we would have won / had won the contract.

❹ The CEO would have promoted me if she had seen / would have seen my presentation.

❺ If we had lowered / would have lowered the price, we would have made more sales.

Speaking exercise This symbol indicates that you should say your answers out loud, then compare them to model recordings included in your audio files.

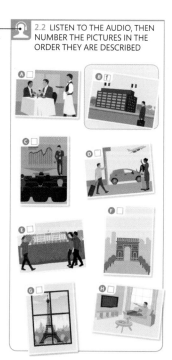

2.2 LISTEN TO THE AUDIO, THEN NUMBER THE PICTURES IN THE ORDER THEY ARE DESCRIBED

Audio

English for Everyone features extensive supporting audio materials. You are encouraged to use them as much as you can, to improve your understanding of spoken English, and to make your own accent and pronunciation more natural. Each file can be played, paused, and repeated as often as you like, until you are confident you understand what has been said.

LISTENING EXERCISES
This symbol indicates that you should listen to an audio track in order to answer the questions in the exercise.

SUPPORTING AUDIO
This symbol indicates that extra audio material is available for you to listen to after completing the module.

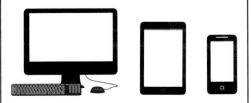

 FREE AUDIO
website and app
www.dkefe.com

Answers

An answers section at the back of the book lists the correct answers for every exercise. Turn to these pages whenever you finish a module and compare your answers with the samples provided, to see how well you have understood each teaching point.

28

28.1 ◄))
1. What is our target this year?
2. Who is handling the account?
3. Who is in charge?
4. What is your sales target?
5. Who responds to complaints?
6. Who spoke to Mr. Jones?
7. What is our plan of action?

Answers Find the answers to every exercise printed at the back of the book.

28.2 ◄))
1. Do I need to dress formally?
2. Did you quote this price?
3. What should I tell the client?
4. Who wants to work in New York?

28.3 ◄))
1. We should increase our margins, **shouldn't we**?
2. I didn't send you the report, **did I**?
3. She'll be a great manager, **won't she**?
4. I'm not getting a raise, **am I**?
5. We haven't made a loss, **have we**?
6. We're going to win the award, **aren't we**?
7. Louis has worked here since 2012, **hasn't he**?
8. Brett worked late last night, **didn't he**?

Exercise numbers Match these numbers to the unique identifier at the top-left corner of each exercise.

28.4 ◄))
1. We could launch our product early, **couldn't we**?
2. Jakob ordered the samples, **didn't he**?
3. We can't cut prices any further, **can we**?
4. We haven't achieved our target, **have we**?
5. We need to improve product quality, **don't we**?

Audio This symbol indicates that the answers can also be listened to.

01 Introductions

When you first join a company, there are many phrases that you can use to introduce yourself. Other people may also use a variety of phrases to introduce you.

⚙ **New language** Present simple and continuous
Aa Vocabulary Etiquette for introductions
🧩 **New skill** Introducing yourself and others

⚙ **1.1 FILL IN THE GAPS USING THE WORDS IN THE PANEL**

How do you _____ _do_ _____ ? I'm Christophe from BlueTech.

1 I'd like to _____ you to Marco from IT.

2 You _____ be Paola from Madrid.

3 Gloria, _____ Julia, our new secretary.

4 Have you two _____ each other before?

5 Great to _____ you again!

6 _____ to meet you, Antonio.

7 Sanjay has _____ me all about you.

8 I don't _____ we've met before, have we?

9 It's a _____ to meet you.

| pleasure | see | ~~do~~ | told | met | must | think | meet | introduce | Nice |

🔊

1.2 MATCH THE BEGINNINGS OF THE INTRODUCTIONS TO THE CORRECT ENDINGS

Peter, Philippe, I'm not sure → if you have met each other.

1. Simone, I'd like to introduce you to
2. Hello. I don't think we've
3. You must be Selma from the
4. Hi, Omar. I think we
5. My boss has told me
6. This is Colin from IT.

Gerald, our new sales manager.

met. My name's Jana.

if you have met each other.

so much about your work.

Colin, meet Liam. He's joining our team soon.

Chicago branch. Great to meet you.

met at the conference in Dubai last year.

1.3 READ THE ARTICLE AND ANSWER THE QUESTIONS

The author says that meeting people is easy.
True ☐ False ☐ Not given ☑

1. Meeting people will always make you successful.
True ☐ False ☐ Not given ☐

2. You should talk about your recent experiences.
True ☐ False ☐ Not given ☐

3. The author thinks food is a good topic of conversation.
True ☐ False ☐ Not given ☐

4. You shouldn't ask how much someone earns.
True ☐ False ☐ Not given ☐

5. The author suggests talking about your education.
True ☐ False ☐ Not given ☐

6. The author says that you shouldn't talk about clients.
True ☐ False ☐ Not given ☐

Meeting and greeting

Meeting new people isn't always easy, but it's an essential skill for a young business professional.

Whether you're looking for a new job, hope to grow your business, or just want to find new clients, you need to talk to the right people. It doesn't always lead to success, but it can provide a great first step. So, what's the best way to start talking?

Talk about your recent experience: "I'm working with some great software engineers at the moment" is a great way to start. You can tell them about your personal life and interests: "I play golf with my friend on the weekend" might be a good starter. But you shouldn't talk about things that are too personal. If you ask someone how much money they earn, they might be offended! Another good idea is to talk about one of your clients: "I often work with ElectroSan, an exciting new Japanese start-up." You will soon find that the person you're talking to wants to know more…

I staying at the hotel on Park Lane all this week.
I'm staying at the hotel on Park Lane all this week.

1 I am catching the train to work at 8:15am each morning.

_____

2 We are having a new printer that is difficult to use.

_____

3 I working at the Guangdong branch all this August.

_____

4 Sanchez is knowing Katie because they worked together.

_____

5 Do you enjoying this presentation? I think it's great.

_____

6 Tim isn't knowing Anna from the Montevideo branch.

_____

7 Marek is liking the new furniture we bought for the office.

_____

8 How are you spelling your name?

_____

9 The meeting usually is take only half an hour.

_____

10 Doug is really enjoy the conference this year.

_____

11 I'd like introduce you to my manager, José Rodriguez.

_____

12 Clara working from 8:30 to 4:30 on Thursdays and Fridays.

_____

Raul ~~presents~~ / is presenting at the moment.

1. Our company is having / have some difficulties at the moment.

2. Pablo, I'd like you to meet / meeting my wife, Elvira.

3. I usually hate conferences, but I enjoy / am enjoying this one a lot.

4. I have / am having two children, a son and a daughter.

5. Michael, I like / I'd like to introduce you to Michelle.

6. I don't think / am not thinking we've met before, have we?

7. It's so great to see / see you again after such a long time.

8. How do you pronounce / are you pronouncing your last name?

9. You must be / being Harold from Copenhagen. Nice to meet you.

10. Hi, I think we met in Oslo, aren't we / didn't we?

02 Getting to know colleagues

Talking about your past work experience is a good way to get to know your colleagues. Past simple and past continuous tenses are often used to do this.

🔧 **New language** Past simple and past continuous
Aa Vocabulary Sharing past experiences
🧩 **New skill** Talking about past experiences

2.1 MARK THE SENTENCES THAT ARE CORRECT

Jan was to look for a new job. ☐
Jan was looking for a new job. ☑

1. I was preparing for the presentation. ☐
   I was prepare for the presentation. ☐

2. Did Greg work in the New York branch? ☐
   Did Greg working in the New York branch? ☐

3. Akira was living in Kyoto in 1998. ☐
   Akira was live in Kyoto in 1998. ☐

4. I didn't understanding the presentation. ☐
   I didn't understand the presentation. ☐

5. Pete was reading a book at 9pm yesterday. ☐
   Pete read a book at 9pm yesterday. ☐

6. I was feeling exhausted at work, so I left. ☐
   I was feel exhausted at work, so I left. ☐

7. Did you enjoy the presentation? ☐
   Did you enjoyed the presentation? ☐

8. Were you worked in IT then? ☐
   Were you working in IT then? ☐

9. Kai wasn't feeling well, so he went home. ☐
   Kai didn't feeling well, so he went home. ☐

10. I was finding a new job in France. ☐
    I found a new job in France. ☐

🔊))

2.2 LISTEN TO THE AUDIO, THEN NUMBER THE PICTURES IN THE ORDER THEY ARE DESCRIBED

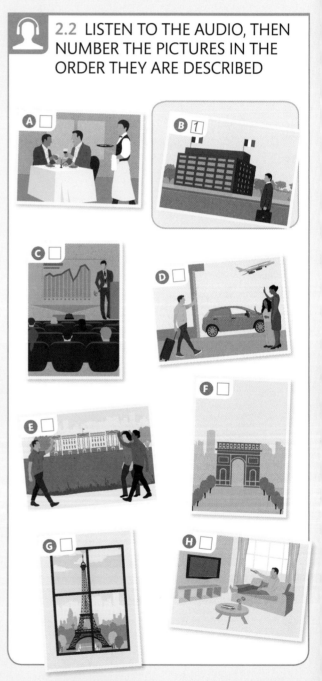

A ☐

B 1

C ☐

D ☐

E ☐

F ☐

G ☐

H ☐

2.3 FILL IN THE GAPS BY PUTTING THE VERBS IN THE PRESENT PERFECT SIMPLE

Chloe _____*has bought*_____ (buy) a new apartment in Paris.

① Daniel _____ (work) for more than five different law firms.

② I _____ (take) the bus to work all my working life.

③ The company _____ (employ) five new people since September.

④ Peter is a terrible waiter. He _____ (start) looking for a different job.

⑤ Andrea _____ (work) here since she graduated in 1999.

⑥ The factory _____ (produce) 15,000 machines this year.

⑦ Tim's really happy. He _____ (finish) his presentation for tomorrow.

⑧ We _____ (sell) our products in more than 25 countries.

⑨ I _____ (walk) to work since my car broke down.

⑩ I _____ (decide) that I'm going to retire next year.

⑪ Dave _____ (take) more time than we expected.

⑫ I _____ (work) at this office for more than 25 years now.

⑬ Chris _____ (visit) more than 50 countries so far.

2.4 MATCH THE BEGINNINGS OF THE SENTENCES TO THE CORRECT ENDINGS

Claire was working for a bank

① Jim was preparing a presentation

② I've worked at this company

③ Chris had to wait for a taxi for

④ Tim moved to New York

⑤ I ran my own software company

⑥ In 2013, our company

for more than ten years.

more than an hour.

when she received a new job offer.

before I started working here.

when his boss entered the room.

bought a smaller Canadian software firm.

when he was transferred to the US office.

 2.5 READ THE ARTICLE AND ANSWER THE QUESTIONS

Silvia has just started work for a bank.
True ☐   False ☐   Not given ☑

① Silvia has worked for three employers so far.
True ☐   False ☐   Not given ☐

② Her first job was boring.
True ☐   False ☐   Not given ☐

③ She worked there for six months.
True ☐   False ☐   Not given ☐

④ Silvia worked in a bar while she was studying.
True ☐   False ☐   Not given ☐

⑤ She only worked in the evenings.
True ☐   False ☐   Not given ☐

⑥ She was working as an intern until recently.
True ☐   False ☐   Not given ☐

Silvia's Blog

HOME | ENTRIES | ABOUT | CONTACT

POSTED FRIDAY, 7:30AM
On the up!

I've just started my new job at Moda Fashions in Edinburgh. I've worked for three different employers so far, and I'm hoping that this job will be the best I've had.

My first job was in a local supermarket. I hated it. I was bored, I had no responsibilities, and the customers were often rude to me. I left after only three months.

After that, I worked in a bar. It was more interesting and I met some interesting people. I was studying for my business diploma while I worked there, so I had something to dream about.

Then I started to become interested in fashion. I was working as an intern for a small fashion agency when I received my job offer. I'm so excited.

2.6 CROSS OUT THE INCORRECT WORDS IN EACH SENTENCE, THEN SAY THE SENTENCES OUT LOUD

My doctor told / ~~was telling~~ me that I should take a vacation.

1 At 3pm yesterday, I discussed / was discussing the new software with our IT team.

2 While Susan has eaten / was eating lunch, her team was working hard.

3 Karl moved to Berlin when he lost / has lost his job in Paris.

4 Alan traveled / was traveling to work when he received a call from his wife.

5 In 2007, I was working / have worked in the company headquarters in Geneva.

6 I have lived / was living in San Francisco since 2003.

7 Peter is sleeping / was sleeping at his desk when his phone rang.

8 They was / have been based in Frankfurt since 1994.

9 While I was living / have living in France, I worked as a waiter.

10 Derek was buying / bought his first house in 2009.

11 What were you doing / have you done at 4pm this afternoon?

12 I was studying / studied in college when I decided to work as a lawyer.

13 Who was in the meeting room when you entered / have entered?

14 We were selling / sold our first machine in China in 2003.

Aa 3.1 DEPARTMENTS WRITE THE DEPARTMENTS FROM THE PANEL UNDER THE CORRECT DEFINITIONS

Deals with buying goods and raw materials

Purchasing

❶ Deals with employee relations and matters such as hiring staff

❷ Ensures that all technological systems are working and maintained

❸ Deals with selling a finished product to outside markets

❹ Deals with maintaining a positive public image for a company

❺ Ensures that all contracts and company activities are legal

❻ Ensures the smooth day-to-day running of the practical aspects of a company

❼ Deals with organization and internal and external communication

❽ Deals with researching and developing future products for a company

❾ Deals with money matters, from paying bills to projecting sales

❿ Deals with promoting products

⓫ Ensures all manufacturing stages run smoothly

Public Relations (PR)   Administration   Research and Development (R&D)   Production

Facilities / Office Services   Accounts / Finance   Information Technology (IT)

Human Resources (HR)   Sales   ~~Purchasing~~   Legal   Marketing

3.2 **ROLES** WRITE THE WORDS FROM THE PANEL
UNDER THE CORRECT PICTURES

employer

① _____

② _____

③ _____

④ _____

⑤ _____

manager

Chief Executive Officer (CEO)

~~employer~~

Chief Financial Officer (CFO)

employee

assistant

Aa 3.3 **DESCRIBING ROLES** WRITE THE PHRASES FROM THE PANEL
UNDER THE CORRECT DEFINITIONS

To ensure something runs smoothly

to look after

① To be employed by a company

_____

② To have a particular job or role

_____

③ To have the duty of ensuring
something is done effectively

_____

④ To have control and authority
over something

_____

⑤ To be employed in a department
or area of an industry

_____

to work as ~~to look after~~ to be in charge of to be responsible for to work in to work for

04 Talking about changes

There are many ways to talk about changes at work in the past and present. Many of the phrases include "used to," which can have several different meanings.

⚙ New language "Used to," "be / get used to"
Aa Vocabulary Small talk
🧩 New skill Talking about changes at work

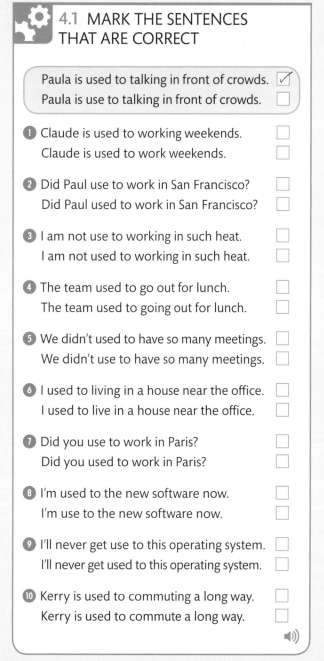

4.1 MARK THE SENTENCES THAT ARE CORRECT

Paula is used to talking in front of crowds. ☑
Paula is use to talking in front of crowds. ☐

1 Claude is used to working weekends. ☐
Claude is used to work weekends. ☐

2 Did Paul use to work in San Francisco? ☐
Did Paul used to work in San Francisco? ☐

3 I am not use to working in such heat. ☐
I am not used to working in such heat. ☐

4 The team used to go out for lunch. ☐
The team used to going out for lunch. ☐

5 We didn't used to have so many meetings. ☐
We didn't use to have so many meetings. ☐

6 I used to living in a house near the office. ☐
I used to live in a house near the office. ☐

7 Did you use to work in Paris? ☐
Did you used to work in Paris? ☐

8 I'm used to the new software now. ☐
I'm use to the new software now. ☐

9 I'll never get use to this operating system. ☐
I'll never get used to this operating system. ☐

10 Kerry is used to commuting a long way. ☐
Kerry is used to commute a long way. ☐

🔊

4.2 LISTEN TO THE AUDIO, THEN NUMBER THE PICTURES IN THE ORDER THEY ARE DESCRIBED

A ☐

B 1

C ☐

D ☐

E ☐

F ☐

G ☐

4.3 REWRITE THE SENTENCES, PUTTING THE WORDS IN THE CORRECT ORDER

working Peter used from to home. is

Peter is used to working from home.

1 to time. We use didn't so have free much

2 get the used on to never I'll left. driving

3 to branch? use Anthony work Did in the Frankfurt

4 get up to I to am having 6am. used at

5 used Derek to isn't so work. commuting far to

6 got new The hasn't to the team system. used operating

7 lunch near used the We to in café park. have the

8 giving Danielle isn't presentations. to used

9 to Pam in branch used work the Cologne. in

10 uniform Phil used a to isn't work. wearing for

4.4 MATCH THE PAIRS OF PHRASES THAT MEAN THE SAME THING

I worked in a bank in the past.	She's not used to working long hours.
1 She doesn't usually work long hours.	I used to work as a doctor.
2 In the past I was a doctor.	I used to work in a bank.
3 Dan's driven on the left for years.	She's used to getting up early.
4 She began getting up early 10 years ago.	I'm not used to spicy food.
5 I tried Indian food once. It's spicy!	Dan's used to driving on the left.
6 I still hate the weather in England after 20 years.	I'm not used to working so late.
7 I don't usually work this late.	We're getting used to the new boss.
8 We've had our new boss for three months.	I'll never get used to English weather.

🔊

4.5 MARK THE BEST REPLY TO EACH STATEMENT

Are you getting used to your new job?
- Yes, but there's a lot to remember. ✓
- Of course I am.

3 Would you like to go for lunch?
- I'm not used to invitations.
- That would be great!

1 Would you like some coffee?
- No, thanks. I'm fine.
- I'm used to drinking tea.

4 Have you seen that new movie?
- I haven't yet. Is it any good?
- Thanks. Tomorrow would be good.

2 You look exhausted, Jenny.
- I'm not used to this hot weather!
- I will sleep later.

5 How was your commute?
- I hate public transportation.
- I'm getting used to the traffic.

🔊

I took a while to get used to / ~~am used to~~ the weather here.

1 Are you used to / got used to living in a tropical country yet?

2 I was used to / used to travel to work on foot before they built the metro.

3 When I lived in Berlin, we used to / get used to live in an apartment downtown.

4 Were you used to / Did you use to work in the Edinburgh branch?

5 I grew up in Japan, so I'm used to / got used to driving on the left.

6 Arnold's used to / use to waking up at 5am every morning.

7 I used to / am used to working for a demanding boss.

8 When I was a child, I didn't get used to / use to like going to school.

9 We are used to / used to go to Florida each year on vacation.

10 My father used to / getting used to work in a factory until it closed down.

Delegating tasks

When things get busy, you may want to delegate tasks to colleagues. To do this, different modal verbs are used in English to show the level of obligation.

⚙ **New language** Modal verbs for obligation
Aa Vocabulary Delegation and politeness
🧩 **New skill** Delegating tasks to colleagues

5.1 MARK THE SENTENCES THAT ARE CORRECT

Peter has to stop working during lunch. ☑
Peter has stop working during lunch. ☐

1. Staff must not smoking in the building. ☐
   Staff must not smoke in the building. ☐

2. We don't have to go to work tomorrow. ☐
   We not have to go to work tomorrow. ☐

3. I have to go home early on Thursday. ☐
   I have going home early on Thursday. ☐

4. You have to do this assignment today. ☐
   You has to do this assignment today. ☐

5. We need increase sales this year. ☐
   We need to increase sales this year. ☐

6. Jim doesn't have to attend the meeting. ☐
   Jim don't have to attend the meeting. ☐

7. The team must not forget their timesheets. ☐
   The team must forget not their timesheets. ☐

8. Paolo has got to signing up for the course. ☐
   Paolo has got to sign up for the course. ☐

9. We will need to hire new staff this fall. ☐
   We will need hiring new staff this fall. ☐

10. We must improve our productivity. ☐
    We must to improve our productivity. ☐

🔊

5.2 LISTEN TO THE AUDIO AND ANSWER THE QUESTIONS

A manager, Janice, is giving tasks to her assistant, James.

Janice is giving a presentation on Wednesday.
True ☐ **False** ☑ **Not given** ☐

1. Janice's presentation is about marketing.
   True ☐ **False** ☐ **Not given** ☐

2. She hasn't reserved a meeting room yet.
   True ☐ **False** ☐ **Not given** ☐

3. Janice wants James to reserve a small room.
   True ☐ **False** ☐ **Not given** ☐

4. She doesn't need a projector or sound system.
   True ☐ **False** ☐ **Not given** ☐

5. Janice needs the room from 2:30 to 5pm.
   True ☐ **False** ☐ **Not given** ☐

6. Janice wants James to email the team.
   True ☐ **False** ☐ **Not given** ☐

7. James should order refreshments for the break.
   True ☐ **False** ☐ **Not given** ☐

8. Janice wants James to check the visuals.
   True ☐ **False** ☐ **Not given** ☐

9. Janice invites James for lunch to say thank you.
   True ☐ **False** ☐ **Not given** ☐

5.3 REWRITE THE SENTENCES, PUTTING THE WORDS IN THE CORRECT ORDER

have | before | to | the | We | presentation | 5pm. | finish

<u>We have to finish the presentation before 5pm.</u>

① copy | you | minutes, | of | please? | give | the | Would | Peter | a

_____

② at | leave | reception. | passes | All | their | must | visitors

_____

③ the | post | to | office, | please? | this | take | Could | letter | you

_____

④ harder | Ramon | to | if | work | he | a promotion. | needs | wants

_____

⑤ needs | the | Sharon | sign up | training | for | course. | to

_____

⑥ copy | you | of | Could | on | leave a | agenda | the | please? | my desk,

_____

⑦ enrolment | before | You | complete | must | the | on | Friday. | form | 5pm

_____

⑧ inside | smoke | Staff | the | must | building. | not

_____

⑨ everyone | Would | you | an email | to | the | send | meeting? | about

_____

⑩ the | by | finish | You | project | must | evening. | Wednesday

_____

◀))

5.4 MATCH THE BEGINNINGS OF THE SENTENCES TO THE CORRECT ENDINGS

Staff must wear	→	identity cards at all times in the building.

Beginnings:
- Staff must wear
1. The company must change
2. I need you to finish
3. Could you keep a
4. Would you inform
5. The company has got to
6. You don't have
7. We need to think

Endings:
- if it wants to survive.
- record of everything you spend this week?
- identity cards at all times in the building.
- the team about the recent changes, please?
- the presentation by Friday.
- about closing some of our branches.
- invest more in training.
- to finish the assignment today.

5.5 READ THE ARTICLE AND ANSWER THE QUESTIONS

The author says delegating is always effective.
True ☐ **False** ☐ **Not given** ✓

1. You should think about who to delegate to.
True ☐ **False** ☐ **Not given** ☐

2. You should follow your team's every step.
True ☐ **False** ☐ **Not given** ☐

3. You should organize team-building activities.
True ☐ **False** ☐ **Not given** ☐

4. Deadlines should always be flexible.
True ☐ **False** ☐ **Not given** ☐

5. Your team won't appreciate negative feedback.
True ☐ **False** ☐ **Not given** ☐

DAILY OFFICE TIPS

A problem shared... can be a problem halved

Getting your fellow team members involved in your daily tasks makes life easier for everyone, surely? But only when you know how to delegate effectively. In my experience, I've found it helps if you think about these four simple steps:

1 You need to think about who you're delegating to. Are they the best person for the job? What will they give, and what will they learn?

2 You don't have to follow your team's every step or decision. But you should be communicative and offer advice. A supported team is an effective team.

3 You must set a clear deadline. Everyone needs to know when the project should end. Otherwise your project will lose its momentum.

4 You have to offer your team feedback. Everyone appreciates credit for success, but they also want to know what went wrong.

5.6 RESPOND OUT LOUD TO THE AUDIO, FILLING IN THE GAPS USING THE WORDS IN THE PANEL

I just received Eric's memo about the conference.

Great. _____*Would*_____ you print me a copy, please?

1 Is this presentation high priority?

No, I _____ you to finish it today.

2 Is it OK if I hand in the report next week?

I'm sorry, Mike. We really _____ have it by Friday.

3 Can we look around the factory?

I'm sorry, but members of the public _____ enter the building.

4 The new uniforms still haven't arrived.

We need them tomorrow. _____ you call the supplier, please?

5 Do you want me to stay late tonight?

No, you _____ to. The deadline is next week.

6 I'm afraid I still haven't finished the report.

Well, I _____ it by 1pm today.

| don't have | need | ~~Would~~ | must | don't need | Could | must not |

06 Vocabulary

Aa 6.1 MONEY AND FINANCE WRITE THE PHRASES FROM THE PANEL UNDER THE CORRECT DEFINITIONS

The amount of money that is available to spend on something

a budget

1 To lose money by spending more than you earn

3 Extra money the bank allows you to spend

4 The regular costs of running a business, such as wages

6 To get into a situation where you owe people money

7 To earn just enough to cover the costs of producing a product

9 Money coming into a business

10 An amount of money spent

12 Records of money paid into and out of a business

13 To fall, especially in worth or value

15 To reach the highest point

16 The amount of one currency that you get when you change it for another

2 To charge less than others who sell the same goods or services as you

_____

5 The amount or value of total sales over a particular period

_____

8 A major decline in economic activity

_____

11 A change to more positive business conditions

_____

14 The rate at which money comes into and goes out of a business

_____

17 To no longer be able to exist as a business

_____

to make a loss   an upturn in the market

sales figures   income

an economic downturn   overheads

the exchange rate   cash flow

an overdraft   to get into debt

to go out of business   to peak

expenditure / outlay   ~~a budget~~

to undercut competitors   to drop

accounts   to break even

31

07 Writing a report

When writing a report, you may need to use different past tenses to show sequences of events. You may also need to use more formal phrasing.

⚙ **New language** Past perfect and past simple
Aa Vocabulary Formal business English
🧩 **New skill** Writing reports

7.1 FILL IN THE GAPS BY PUTTING THE VERBS IN THE PAST PERFECT OR PAST SIMPLE

We ___*stayed*___ (stay) in the hotel that our client ___*had recommended*___ (recommend) to us.

1 Sales _____ (be) good because we _____ (organize) a good marketing campaign.

2 Sales _____ (fall) sharply, so we _____ (decide) to withdraw the product.

3 Aditya _____ (want) to try a program that the team _____ (not use) before.

4 After Peter _____ (finish) the report, he _____ (want) to go on vacation.

🔊

7.2 CROSS OUT THE INCORRECT WORDS IN EACH SENTENCE

Sandra **gave** / ~~had given~~ a presentation that she ~~prepared~~ / had prepared two years ago.

1 Ramon **wrote** / had written ten pages of the report when his computer **crashed** / had crashed.

2 Many of our employees **did not** / had not visited the factory before and **were** / had been very impressed.

3 Bob's speech **was** / had been disappointing because he **didn't prepare** / hadn't prepared well.

4 Nobody **told** / had told the conference delegates where their hotel **was** / had been.

5 I **didn't delegate** / hadn't delegated tasks to Kai before, but I **thought** / had thought he did a good job.

🔊

7.3 REWRITE THE SENTENCES, CORRECTING THE ERRORS

> The purpose of this report is review our advertising campaign for next year.
> _The purpose of this report is to review our advertising campaign for next year._

1 The followed report will explore our new sales strategy.

_____

2 As can be seeing in the table, we have invested $4 million this year.

_____

3 Some of our customers have stating that they are not satisfied with the result.

_____

4 Our initial investigation suggestion that this is not true.

_____

5 Our beginning recommendation is to reduce the budget by 50 percent.

_____

6 We consulting a number of focus groups for this report.

_____

◀))

Aa 7.4 MATCH THE BEGINNINGS OF THE SENTENCES TO THE CORRECT ENDINGS

We consulted a number	is to review our current sales strategy.
1 The purpose of our report	we should invest more in R&D.
2 The following report presents	of focus groups for this report.
3 Our clients stated that	proceed with the sale of the subsidiary.
4 Based on the initial research,	a summary of our findings.
5 Our principal recommendation is to	they were unhappy with the changes.

◀))

33

LOCATION REPORT

The aim of this report is to assess the advantages and disadvantages of moving the company headquarters to Alchester. The following report will look at location, transportation, housing, and the available tax breaks.

Location The site in Alchester is 20 miles from downtown. The town has two large colleges and a number of other IT companies. However, it is more than 200 miles to the nearest major city.

Transportation There is an airport and the rail connections to other cities are good. However, the airport is far (30 miles away) and the station can only be reached by taxi.

Housing Based on the initial research, we concluded that housing is much more affordable than in major cities. The proposed site is near an attractive suburb.

Tax subsidies The local government offers large grants to companies that want to move to the area. However, these are only available if the company is willing to stay in the area for more than ten years.

Conclusion Many of our employees stated that they would not be happy living so far from a city. Others stated that they found the affordable accommodation very attractive. The grants offered are attractive, but the company will need to make a big commitment.

What does the report aim to assess?

The company's profits for the year ☐
A potential new location for the company ☑
The company's current location ☐

1 Where is the site in Alchester?

20 miles from downtown ☐
200 miles from downtown ☐
Downtown ☐

2 What is good about the transportation links?

The location of the station ☐
The location of the airport ☐
Rail connections to other cities ☐

3 What are the findings about housing?

It is affordable in Alchester ☐
The company is still researching it ☐
The suburbs are not attractive ☐

4 What must companies do to get a tax subsidy?

Move to Alchester ☐
Stay in Alchester for over ten years ☐
Work with the local government ☐

5 What is the conclusion of the report?

The company will move to Alchester ☐
The company won't move to Alchester ☐
A decision has not yet been made ☐

7.6 MARK THE SENTENCES THAT ARE CORRECT

As can be see in the table, our profits have declined by 9 percent this year. ☐
As can be seen in the table, our profits have declined by 9 percent this year. ☑

❶ The purpose of this report is to compare the two factories. ☐
The purpose of this report is compare the two factories. ☐

❷ Focus groups had been consulted before we implemented the policy. ☐
Focus groups had be consulted before we implemented the policy. ☐

❸ Sales of our products are fallen in comparison with the previous quarter. ☐
Sales of our products had fallen in comparison with the previous quarter. ☐

❹ Our principal recommendation is to increase investment in R&D. ☐
Our principal recommendation is increase investment in R&D. ☐

❺ Profits had risen by more than 20 percent in the first half of 2015. ☐
Profits had risen with more than 20 percent in the first half of 2015. ☐

🔊

7.7 FILL IN THE GAPS USING THE WORDS IN THE PANEL

CLOSED We closed the branch after our costs had _____*risen*_____ by more than 20 percent.

❶ In this report we will _____ the findings of our research.

❷ The _____ of this report is to investigate the pros and cons of the new software.

❸ This bar chart _____ the sales figures for the last two years.

❹ Our customers _____ that they had been disappointed with the product.

| purpose | stated | compares | ~~risen~~ | present |

🔊

35

08 Making apologies

The present perfect continuous describes ongoing situations in the past that may affect the present. It can be used in apologies and to give reasons for problems.

⚙ **New language** Present perfect continuous
Aa Vocabulary Apologies
🧩 **New skill** Apologizing on the telephone

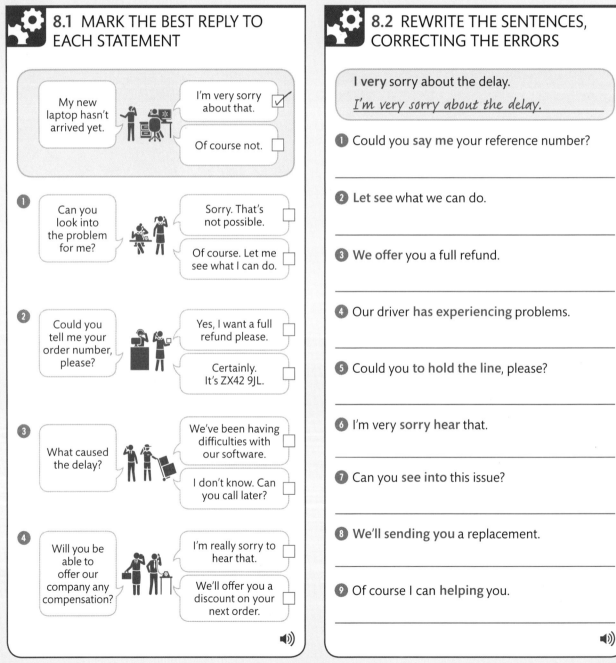

8.1 MARK THE BEST REPLY TO EACH STATEMENT

My new laptop hasn't arrived yet.

- I'm very sorry about that. ✓
- Of course not. ☐

①
Can you look into the problem for me?

- Sorry. That's not possible. ☐
- Of course. Let me see what I can do. ☐

②
Could you tell me your order number, please?

- Yes, I want a full refund please. ☐
- Certainly. It's ZX42 9JL. ☐

③
What caused the delay?

- We've been having difficulties with our software. ☐
- I don't know. Can you call later? ☐

④
Will you be able to offer our company any compensation?

- I'm really sorry to hear that. ☐
- We'll offer you a discount on your next order. ☐

8.2 REWRITE THE SENTENCES, CORRECTING THE ERRORS

I very sorry about the delay.
I'm very sorry about the delay.

① Could you **say me** your reference number?

_____

② **Let see** what we can do.

_____

③ **We offer** you a full refund.

_____

④ Our driver **has experiencing** problems.

_____

⑤ Could you **to hold the line**, please?

_____

⑥ I'm very **sorry hear** that.

_____

⑦ Can you **see into** this issue?

_____

⑧ **We'll sending you** a replacement.

_____

⑨ Of course I can **helping** you.

_____

🔊

🔊

8.3 FILL IN THE GAPS USING THE PHRASES IN THE PANEL

Can you _____*look into*_____ the problem for me?

1. I'm very _____ to hear that, sir.

2. Certainly. Let's _____ what I can do.

3. Could you tell me your _____ number, please?

4. Could you please _____ the line?

5. I'm sorry. Our IT system's been _____ difficulties.

6. My order _____ dirty and broken.

7. Can you _____ any compensation?

8. Of course. We'll give you a _____ on your next order.

reference
hold
sorry
~~look into~~
offer
experiencing
discount
see
arrived

8.4 CROSS OUT THE INCORRECT WORD IN EACH SENTENCE, THEN SAY THE SENTENCES OUT LOUD

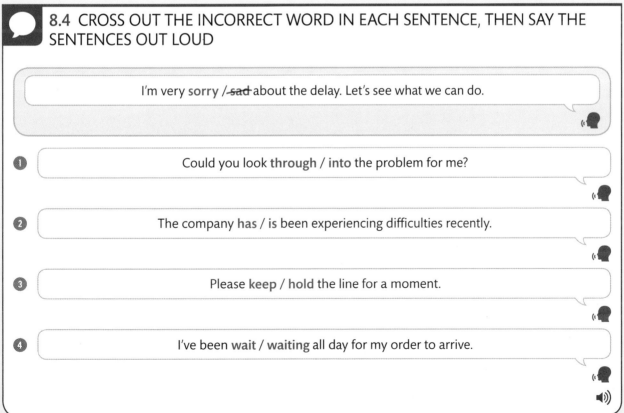

I'm very **sorry** / ~~sad~~ about the delay. Let's see what we can do.

1. Could you look **through** / **into** the problem for me?

2. The company **has** / **is** been experiencing difficulties recently.

3. Please **keep** / **hold** the line for a moment.

4. I've been **wait** / **waiting** all day for my order to arrive.

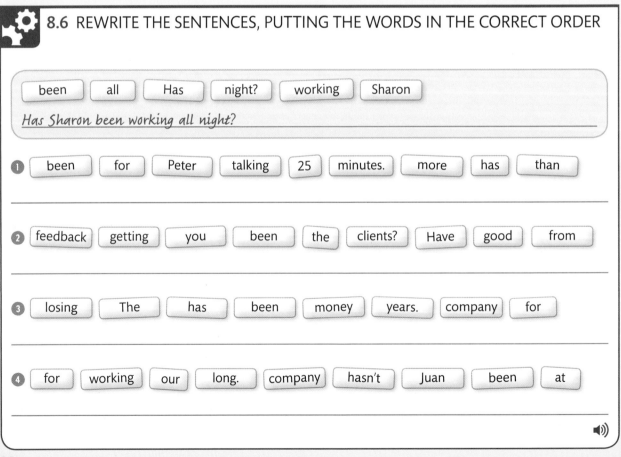

8.5 FILL IN THE GAPS BY PUTTING THE VERBS IN THE PRESENT PERFECT CONTINUOUS

Katherine _____ *has been waiting* _____ (wait) for her feedback from the interview.

1. We _____ (prepare) a proposal all evening.

2. Our website _____ (experience) difficulties this morning.

3. Chris _____ (work) on that project for three months now.

4. Our products _____ (not sell) well so far this year.

8.6 REWRITE THE SENTENCES, PUTTING THE WORDS IN THE CORRECT ORDER

| been | all | Has | night? | working | Sharon |

Has Sharon been working all night?

1. | been | for | Peter | talking | 25 | minutes. | more | has | than |

_____

2. | feedback | getting | you | been | the | clients? | Have | good | from |

_____

3. | losing | The | has | been | money | years. | company | for |

_____

4. | for | working | our | long. | company | hasn't | Juan | been | at |

_____

8.7 LISTEN TO THE AUDIO, THEN NUMBER THE SENTENCES IN THE ORDER YOU HEAR THEM

Jock Douglas calls his suppliers to ask about an order that he's expecting.

Ⓐ I've been waiting for three weeks now, so I'm not at all happy. ☐

Ⓑ Could you tell me your order reference number? ☐

Ⓒ We would like to offer you a gift voucher worth $100. ☐

Ⓓ Could you please hold the line one moment? ☐

Ⓔ I'm really sorry to hear that, Mr. Douglas. ☐1

Ⓕ Your order was dispatched yesterday. ☐

8.8 READ THE EMAIL AND MARK THE CORRECT SUMMARY

❶ The wrong model of laptop arrived. This happened because of a software problem at the warehouse. The company has offered a 10 percent discount on the next order. ☐

❷ The wrong model of printer arrived. This happened because of a software problem at the warehouse. The company has offered a 40 percent discount on the next order. ☐

❸ The wrong model of software arrived. This happened because of a flood at the warehouse. The company has offered a 25 percent discount on the next order. ☐

❹ The wrong model of laptop arrived. This happened because of a software upgrade at the warehouse. The company has offered a 25 percent discount on the next order. ☐

✉ ∨ ✕

To: Mario Grando

Subject: Your order

Dear Mario Grando,

Thank you for your email regarding your order dated August 4th. I am very sorry to hear that the wrong model of laptop arrived, and we apologize for the inconvenience this caused. I've been looking into the problem and see that you received model A147 instead of A149. We've been upgrading the software in our warehouse recently, and, unfortunately, last week we were unable to fulfill all our orders correctly. As an apology, however, we'd like to offer you a refund of 25 percent off your next order with our company. I've attached the voucher to this email.

Best regards,
Mohammed Ahmed

↩ ↩↩   𝌆 🗑

09 Vocabulary

Aa 9.1 COMMUNICATION TECHNOLOGY WRITE THE PHRASES FROM THE PANEL UNDER THE CORRECT DEFINITIONS

Computer programs

software

1 Internet-based tools for communicating with friends and communities

_____

3 Computerized; not operated by a human

_____

4 To enter or connect to something

_____

6 Current and modern

_____

7 Easy for the operator to use

_____

9 A group conversation held by phone

_____

10 Losing a phone or internet connection

_____

12 A small computing device, such as a smartphone or tablet, that is easily carried

_____

13 To work without an internet connection

_____

15 To connect a mobile device to electricity to give it more power

_____

16 A name and code used to access an account on a computing device

_____

2 A collection of linked pages accessed through the internet

_____

5 To work with an internet connection

_____

8 To save an extra copy of a document in case the original is lost

_____

11 To get an application from the internet onto a device or computer

_____

14 An email has been automatically returned without reaching the intended recipient

_____

17 A system of interconnected technology

_____

social media

to download an app

a username and password

to work offline

to charge   a website

to access

automated   to back up

an email has bounced

up to date

a mobile device   user-friendly

~~software~~   a network

to work online

breaking up

a conference call

🔊

10 Making plans by email

English uses a variety of phrases to make and check plans with co-workers by email. It is important to ensure that even informal messages are polite.

⚙ **New language** Email language
Aa Vocabulary Meetings and workshops
🧩 **New skill** Making plans

10.1 MATCH THE BEGINNINGS OF THE SENTENCES TO THE CORRECT ENDINGS

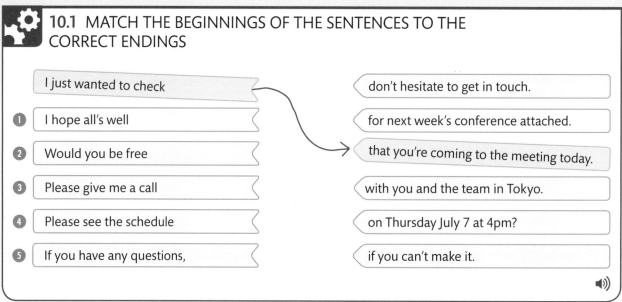

I just wanted to check ——→ that you're coming to the meeting today.

1 I hope all's well → don't hesitate to get in touch.

2 Would you be free → for next week's conference attached.

3 Please give me a call → with you and the team in Tokyo.

4 Please see the schedule → on Thursday July 7 at 4pm?

5 If you have any questions, → if you can't make it.

🔊

10.2 FILL IN THE GAPS USING THE WORDS IN THE PANEL

I just wanted to _____check_____ that you're attending this week's meeting.

1 I was _____ if you could help me prepare my presentation.

2 Would you be free to _____ on Thursday evening?

3 I'm _____ Sanjay and Anita in on this email.

4 I _____ all's well with you and the team in Delhi.

5 Please see the minutes of yesterday's meeting _____ .

6 If you have any _____ , please let me know.

7 How _____ joining us at the pizza place later this evening?

about
hope
meet
questions
~~check~~
copying
wondering
attached

🔊

10.3 REWRITE THE SENTENCES, CORRECTING THE ERRORS

I hope all well with you and the team.
I hope all's well with you and the team.

1 I just wanted check that you're coming to the presentation.

_____

2 Would you free next Wednesday morning at 11:30?

_____

3 Please find a copy of the report attach.

_____

4 If you any questions, please let me know.

_____

5 I'm copy Ricardo in on this.

_____

10.4 READ THE EMAIL AND MARK THE CORRECT SUMMARY

1 Jerome wants to meet tomorrow to discuss the new software package. He has asked Claude to send him the timetable. ☐

2 Jerome is inviting Françoise and Claude to come to software training in Room 3. ☐

3 Jerome is emailing to check that Claude is coming to the IT meeting. Françoise has sent the agenda and a memo. ☐

4 Jerome is inviting Françoise to a meeting with the IT team. He has sent Françoise and Claude a copy of the agenda. ☐

To: Françoise Thomas
Subject: Software package

Hi Françoise,
I hope all's well with you and the team. I just wanted to check that you got the email I sent yesterday about the new software package that goes live on Thursday. Claude and I want to meet the IT department tomorrow morning to discuss it. Would you be free to join us in meeting room 3 at 9:30am? Please find attached an agenda and memo about the software specifications. I've copied Claude in on this message. If you have any questions, please let me know.
Best regards,
Jerome

11 Keeping clients informed

Use the present continuous to inform clients about current situations and future arrangements. Continuous tenses can also soften questions and requests.

⚙ **New language** Continuous tenses
Aa Vocabulary Arrangements and schedules
🧩 **New skill** Keeping clients informed

⚙ 11.1 REWRITE THE PRESENT CONTINUOUS SENTENCES, CORRECTING THE ERRORS

I **are hoping** to finish my report on July's sales later today.

I am hoping to finish my report on July's sales later today.

1. Mohammed **is meet** the new supplier to discuss a new deal.

_____

2. Jola **is talk** to Sales this afternoon to agree new discounts.

_____

3. They **is aiming** to have the presentation ready by 5:00pm.

_____

4. I **am writeing** to inform you that there is a delay with the part you need.

_____

5. We **still are waiting** to hear from the Chinese partners.

_____

🔊

🎧 11.2 LISTEN TO THE AUDIO AND MARK WHETHER THE ACTIVITY IN EACH PICTURE TAKES PLACE IN THE PRESENT OR THE FUTURE

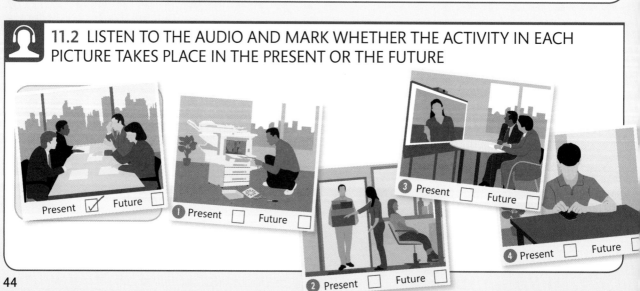

Present ✓ Future ☐

1. Present ☐ Future ☐

2. Present ☐ Future ☐

3. Present ☐ Future ☐

4. Present ☐ Future ☐

Aa 11.3 READ THE CLUES AND WRITE THE WORDS FROM THE PANEL IN THE CORRECT PLACES ON THE GRID

¹h e s i t ⁶a t e

ACROSS

1 To pause

2 To get

3 To make something definite

DOWN

4 To tell

5 To like more

6 To promise

assure   obtain   confirm   ~~hesitate~~   prefer   inform

11.4 MARK THE MOST POLITE SENTENCE IN EACH PAIR

You need to extend the deadline. ☐
I was wondering if you would consider extending the deadline. ☑

1 Are you going to the new product launch? ☐
Will you be attending the launch of the new products? ☐

2 I was wondering if we could put our meeting back to tomorrow. ☐
Can we put our meeting back to tomorrow? ☐

3 We want to send new designs by Friday. ☐
We are aiming to send the new designs by Friday. ☐

4 Will you be paying for the order in cash or by card? ☐
Will you pay in cash or by card? ☐

5 I was wondering if you would take the clients out for dinner. ☐
Will you take the clients out for dinner? ☐

11.5 REWRITE THE SENTENCES, PUTTING THE WORDS IN THE CORRECT ORDER

we | laptop. | I | if | borrow | could | your | was | wondering

I was wondering if we could borrow your laptop.

1. final | the | We | report. | still | sales | putting | are | together

_____

2. tomorrow's | you | presentation | be | Will | conference? | the | giving | at

_____

3. postpone | were | if | We | could | meeting. | wondering | we | our

_____

11.6 READ THE EMAIL AND ANSWER THE QUESTIONS

Sanjay's project is running on time.
True ☐ **False** ☐ **Not given** ☑

1. Sanjay wants to meet the suppliers.
True ☐ **False** ☐ **Not given** ☐

2. The new designs for the fabric are complex.
True ☐ **False** ☐ **Not given** ☐

3. The fabrics will be delivered in two weeks' time.
True ☐ **False** ☐ **Not given** ☐

4. Sanjay offers Fiona compensation.
True ☐ **False** ☐ **Not given** ☐

To: Fiona McRae

Subject: Project update

Dear Fiona,

I was wondering if we could have a brief project update meeting as the project is running late. Unfortunately, the new designs for the fabric that we plan to launch have proved more complicated to print than we initially thought. The suppliers in Bangladesh have informed us that the final printed materials will be with us at the end of this month, not in two weeks as per our order.

The suppliers have told us they will work around the clock to minimize the delay, and they apologize for any inconvenience this may cause us.

Yours truly,
Sanjay

12 Informal communication

Phrasal verbs have two or more parts. They are often used in informal spoken and written English, in things such as messages and requests to co-workers.

⚙ **New language** Phrasal verbs
Aa Vocabulary Arrangements and plans
New skill Keeping co-workers informed

12.1 CROSS OUT THE INCORRECT WORDS IN EACH SENTENCE

 Is the printer jammed again? I'll ask Dave to look **into** / ~~out~~ / ~~up~~ it.

1 Can you deal **with** / **at** / **out** the cleaners, please? The kitchen is a mess.

2 Can we catch **on** / **up** / **off** later this morning at around 11:00?

3 Is the fridge broken again? I'll **catch** / **deal** / **look** into that now.

4 Have we run **on** / **out** / **in** of paper? There's none in the photocopier.

◀))

12.2 FILL IN THE GAPS USING THE PHRASAL VERBS IN THE PANEL

Let's _____*catch up*_____ now you're back from your vacation.

1 Can we _____ a meeting with Marketing and Sales?

2 Have you asked Surina to _____ all the paperwork?

3 The printer has _____ of ink again.

4 I can't _____ what Dave wants me to do.

5 I need to _____ the topic of punctuality with you.

| figure out | bring up | fix up | ~~catch up~~ | fill out | run out |

◀))

12.3 REWRITE THE SENTENCES BY CHANGING THE POSITION OF THE PARTICLE

> Can you **fill out** that form?
> *Can you fill that form out?*

1 I need to **back up** my files.

_____

2 Can you **give out** the agenda?

_____

3 Can we **call off** tomorrow's meeting?

_____

4 Can you **pass on** my message to her?

_____

5 Let me **hand out** the minutes.

_____

6 I want to **put on** my tie.

_____

7 Can you **fix up** another meeting?

_____

8 I need to **send out** an email.

_____

9 We are **taking on** new staff.

_____

10 Can you **set up** the projector?

_____

11 I'd like to **talk over** the sales plan.

_____

◀))

12.4 LISTEN TO THE AUDIO AND ANSWER THE QUESTIONS

It is Jack's first day back at work after his vacation. His co-worker Amanda calls him.

> Why is Amanda calling Jack?
> **To arrange a meeting** ☐
> **To cancel a meeting** ☑
> **To place some orders** ☐

1 What is the problem with Amanda's files?
She hasn't backed them up ☐
She has deleted them ☐
Some of them are missing ☐

2 When does Jack set up a meeting with Amanda?
Thursday morning ☐
Thursday afternoon ☐
Friday morning ☐

3 What does Amanda want Jack to do?
Call customers about their feedback ☐
Deal with new customers ☐
Write a report about feedback ☐

4 What does Jack offer to do?
Delegate some of Amanda's emails ☐
Delete some of Amanda's emails ☐
Deal with some of Amanda's emails ☐

5 What does Amanda ask Jack to pass on?
A message ☐
A package ☐
A sales report ☐

6 What will Jack wear for his site visit?
His best suit ☐
His best tie ☐
His best suit and tie ☐

Can you pass a message **on** / ~~up~~ / ~~off~~ to Syed? I can't make this afternoon's meeting. 🗣

❶ Jamil's flight is delayed. I think we'll have to call our meeting with him **in** / **off** / **out**. 🗣

❷ All employees have to put an apron **in** / **up** / **on** before entering the kitchen. 🗣

❸ We're hoping to give **off** / **out** / **in** samples of our work at the exhibition. 🗣

❹ It's really important to back your files **over** / **on** / **up** every night or you could lose work. 🗣

🔊

⚙️ **12.6 FILL IN THE GAPS USING THE PHRASES IN THE PANEL**

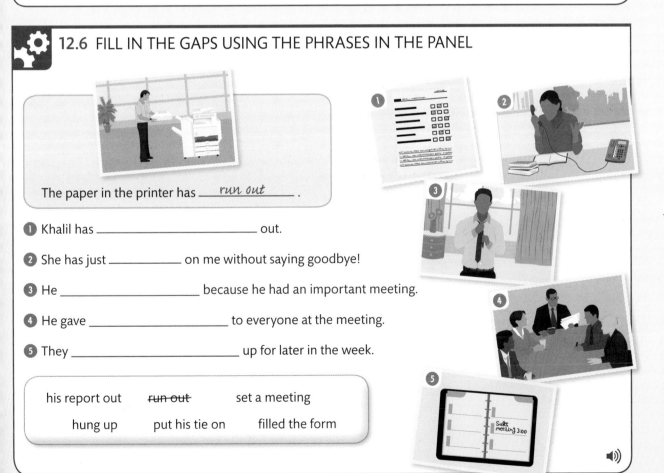

The paper in the printer has ___*run out*___ .

❶ Khalil has _____ out.

❷ She has just _____ on me without saying goodbye!

❸ He _____ because he had an important meeting.

❹ He gave _____ to everyone at the meeting.

❺ They _____ up for later in the week.

his report out	~~run out~~	set a meeting
hung up	put his tie on	filled the form

🔊

13 Vocabulary

Aa 13.1 PRODUCTION WRITE THE PHRASES FROM THE PANEL UNDER THE CORRECT DEFINITIONS

Systems that ensure that products are of a high standard

quality control

1 The external wrapping of goods before they are sold

3 Made by a person without the use of a machine

4 Something that is made or produced only once

6 Goods that a company has made but not yet sold

7 A declaration that a product meets certain standards and is suitable for sale

9 The first form of a design that can be changed, copied, or developed

10 A line of people or machinery in a factory, each making a specific part of a product

12 Moving goods from one place to another

13 Found or bought in a morally acceptable way

15 A building or group of buildings where goods are made

16 The process of making large numbers of goods, usually in a factory

2 A process to check that goods meet certain standards

_____

5 Requiring a lot of human effort to make something

_____

8 The basic substances that are used to make a product

_____

11 A place where goods are stored before being shipped to customers or sellers

_____

14 Manufacturing too much of something in relation to demand

_____

17 A company that provides or supplies another company with goods and services

_____

packaging   labor-intensive

mass production   shipping

ethically sourced   handmade

raw materials   a one-off production

~~quality control~~   overproduction

stock   product approval

a factory   a prototype

a warehouse   product testing

a supplier   a production line

51

14 Describing a process

The passive voice can be useful when you need to describe how a process works. It places emphasis on the action rather than the person or thing doing it.

 New language The passive voice
Aa Vocabulary Processes and manufacturing
New skill Discussing how things are done

14.1 CROSS OUT THE INCORRECT WORDS IN EACH SENTENCE

Our soaps **are made** / ~~maked~~ using the finest French lavender.

1 The media **had been** / **have** told about the press launch and were out in force.

2 New models **are been** / **are being** created to coincide with the premiere of the movie.

3 The design has been **patent** / **patented** so nobody can copy it.

4 Our coffee is **producing** / **produced** using the finest coffee beans from Kenya.

5 It is thought that the sandwich **was** / **were** invented in 1762.

14.2 LISTEN TO THE AUDIO AND NUMBER THE PICTURES IN THE ORDER THEY ARE DESCRIBED

A ☐

B 1

C ☐
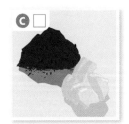

D ☐

E ☐

F ☐

G ☐

H ☐

14.3 REWRITE THE SENTENCES USING THE PASSIVE VOICE

> Our distribution team sends out our products from our warehouse in Michigan.
> _Our products are sent out from our warehouse in Michigan by our distribution team._

1 A separate department audits our accounts every May.

_____

2 Our professional coffee tasters approve the coffee blends we produce.

_____

3 Security staff scan all passengers' luggage when they go through Departures.

_____

4 Jane designs all our marketing material for the Asia office.

_____

5 Our packing department checks all the orders before delivery.

_____

6 Stephen updates the database with customers' details.

_____

7 Our cosmetics buyer buys all our ingredients from Fair Trade suppliers.

_____

8 Nicola adds new lines to our women's fashion range on a regular basis.

_____

9 Jason invented the new product tracking app for customers.

_____

10 Our marketing team launched our new website in January.

_____

◀))

14.4 READ THE ARTICLE AND ANSWER THE QUESTIONS

Bread was invented in modern times.
True ☐ **False** ☑ **Not given** ☐

1 Bread is not eaten in many cultures.
True ☐ **False** ☐ **Not given** ☐

2 Yeast is added to the dough after kneading.
True ☐ **False** ☐ **Not given** ☐

3 The dough is kneaded for about 10 minutes.
True ☐ **False** ☐ **Not given** ☐

4 Different countries have different shapes of bread.
True ☐ **False** ☐ **Not given** ☐

5 The dough is left to rise two times before it is baked.
True ☐ **False** ☐ **Not given** ☐

FOOD TODAY

The stuff of life

This week we look at how bread is made throughout the world.

Bread has been made since prehistoric times and is eaten by most cultures today. But how is it made? A raising agent like yeast is added to flour with warm water. A dough is made and the gluten in the flour is activated by a process called kneading, which is when the dough is massaged for about 10 minutes. The dough is then left in a warm place to rise. Then the air is knocked out of it and it is kneaded a second time. The dough is then shaped into a loaf or rolls. Some of these are very decorative, and individual bakers often have their own special design. Finally, the dough is left to rise again and then baked in a hot oven. The result is delicious warm bread!

14.5 MATCH THE ACTIVE SENTENCES TO THE PASSIVE SENTENCES WITH THE SAME MEANING

We must beat our competitors' prices.

1 They can't have checked these toys.

2 She should have given them a discount.

3 Freya can't have taken the order.

4 We can give every customer a free bag.

5 We shouldn't ignore faults in the products.

6 You can't beat our prices.

7 He must have placed his order late.

The order can't have been taken by her.

Our prices can't be beaten.

Our competitors' prices must be beaten.

These toys can't have been checked.

Faults in the products shouldn't be ignored.

A free bag can be given to every customer.

His order must have been placed late.

A discount should have been given.

🔊

54

14.6 LOOK AT THE DIAGRAM AND SAY THE SENTENCES OUT LOUD, FILLING IN THE GAPS USING THE WORDS IN THE PANEL

How It's Made

Learn how our cakes are baked.

First, a cake recipe _____is chosen_____ by the cake-maker.

1 Next, the ingredients _____ together to make a cake mixture.

2 Then the cake mixture _____ into cake pans.

3 Next, the cakes _____ in a hot oven.

4 When the cakes are cooked, they _____ out of the oven.

5 The cakes _____ to cool on a wire cooling rack.

6 Finally, the cakes _____ and decorated with icing.

are taken	are mixed	~~is chosen~~	is poured
are assembled	are left		are put

55

15 Describing a product

When describing a product, you will usually use adjectives. You can use more than one adjective, but they must be in a particular order.

✿ **New language** Adjective order
Aa Vocabulary Opinion and fact adjectives
✦ **New skill** Describing a product

15.1 WRITE THE WORDS FROM THE PANEL IN THE CORRECT GROUPS

OPINION	SIZE	AGE	COLOR	NATIONALITY	MATERIAL
fantastic					

magenta   ancient   Indian   ~~fantastic~~   huge   Turkish   modern   tiny   leather   amazing
metal   Chinese   crimson   excellent   large   black   state-of-the-art   plastic

15.2 REWRITE THE SENTENCES, PUTTING THE WORDS IN THE CORRECT ORDER

new   at   amazing   necklace!   this   Look   gold

Look at this amazing new gold necklace!

① Indian   It's   by   designer.   fabulous,   young   made   a

_____

② I   bowls.   these   small,   china   blue   fantastic,   love

_____

③ outstanding   launching   an   new   clothes.   We're   of   range

_____

🔊

I really like the new red / ~~diamond~~ velvet sofas around the office.

1 What a lovely plastic / stylish desk you have!

2 Sam asked me to design a silver / classic brown chair.

3 I brought back some delicious china / Turkish candy from my trip.

4 Do you like this pretty / paper crimson watch for ladies?

5 Do you like our cute green / ugly teddy bear for our new children's range?

6 Our competitors are selling unfashionable / intelligent black suits.

7 Our team is developing an innovative leather / popular interior for our executive car.

8 I love buying large awesome / yellow flowers for the office.

9 Jane has bought an expensive / friendly classic car at an auction.

10 We have an amazing cotton / Italian coffee machine in our office.

11 I have ordered some of those fabulous leather / double-sided business cards.

12 We have an amazing awful / gray oven in our staff kitchen.

13 This is our new lightweight / comfortable digital camera.

15.4 LISTEN TO THE AUDIO AND MARK WHICH THINGS ARE DESCRIBED

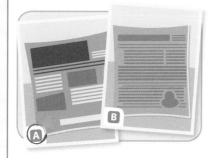

15.5 READ THE ARTICLE AND ANSWER THE QUESTIONS

Dress Right only sells clothes for men and women.
True ☐ **False** ☑ **Not given** ☐

1 The new range of clothing is mainly beige.
True ☐ **False** ☐ **Not given** ☐

2 Dress Right sells fashionable clothes.
True ☐ **False** ☐ **Not given** ☐

3 The new denim range is ground-breaking.
True ☐ **False** ☐ **Not given** ☐

4 Dress Right only sells uniforms in one set of colors.
True ☐ **False** ☐ **Not given** ☐

5 Dress Right is having fashion shows in all its stores.
True ☐ **False** ☐ **Not given** ☐

FASHION AND STYLE

Dress Right for all occasions

We have everything you need to dress the family in style, whether it is for school, work, a trip or a special event. Want to know what is new? We have kept our trademark stylish, modern, and colorful style in our new range of clothing. You'll find the usual brown and red clothes as well as fashionable, new bags and shoes. In the Directions collection, there are fabulous, trend-setting styles for both men and women. In addition to this, we are also launching an innovative, modern, denim range of casual wear.

This year also sees the launch of practical, hard-wearing school clothes in a range of colors. So come and see what Dress Right can do for you in a store near you or online.

15.6 SAY THE SENTENCES OUT LOUD, FILLING IN THE GAPS USING THE WORDS IN THE PANEL

We offer good, _cheap_ food that people can afford.

7 My dad drives a _____ , black truck.

1 Their website is easy to use because it has a _____ , effective style.

8 Ella makes high-quality, _____ curtains.

2 Zander's Pizzeria makes _____ , oven-baked pizzas.

9 We aim to give _____ customer service.

3 I love this _____ , leather armchair.

10 We offer a _____ , personal experience.

4 The new, _____ brochure is very bright and attractive.

11 I don't like those ugly, _____ desks. They're hideous!

5 I like the _____ , new rooms in that hotel.

12 This modern, _____ car is much faster than my old one.

6 Those small, _____ earrings are beautiful.

13 What a _____ , big photo of all the team!

| huge | cotton | full-color | clean | delicious | ~~cheap~~ | Japanese |
| unique | simple | gorgeous | comfortable | diamond | excellent | wooden |

59

16 Vocabulary

Aa **16.1** **MARKETING AND ADVERTISING** WRITE THE WORDS FROM THE PANEL UNDER THE CORRECT PICTURES

direct mail

1 _____

2 _____

3 _____

6 _____

7 _____

8 _____

9 _____

12 _____

13 _____

14 _____

15 _____

18 _____

19 _____

20 _____

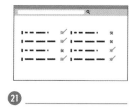

21 _____

④ _____

⑤ _____

⑩ _____

⑪ _____

⑯ _____

⑰ _____

㉒ _____

㉓ _____

advertising agency   slogan / tagline

copywriter   online survey   leaflet / flyer

door-to-door sales   logo   brand

radio advertising   promote

merchandise   poster   consumer

television advertising   sales pitch

~~direct mail~~   billboard   word of mouth

free sample   coupons

unique selling point / USP   sponsor

market research   social media

🔊

17 Marketing a product

You can use a variety of adjectives and adverbs to describe the key features when marketing a product or service. Not all adjectives can be modified in the same way.

New language Adjectives and adverbs
Aa Vocabulary Descriptive adjectives
New skill Modifying descriptions of products

17.1 WRITE THE WORDS FROM THE PANEL IN THE CORRECT GROUPS

EXTREME	ABSOLUTE	CLASSIFYING
enormous	true	metal

electronic   terrible   wrong   brilliant   furious   ~~enormous~~   scientific   woolen   perfect   fascinating

equal   ~~true~~   impossible   industrial   exhausted   organic   ~~metal~~   unique   empty   rural   awful

17.2 MARK THE SENTENCES THAT ARE CORRECT

The test was absolutely impossible. ☑
The test was fairly impossible. ☐

❶ The factory was totally destroyed. ☐
The factory was very destroyed. ☐

❷ I was thoroughly tired this morning. ☐
I was thoroughly exhausted this morning. ☐

❸ The warehouse is almost empty. ☐
The warehouse is very empty. ☐

❹ Jon is an absolutely good speaker. ☐
Jon is an extremely good speaker. ☐

❺ Peter is nearly good at Spanish. ☐
Peter is fairly good at Spanish. ☐

❻ The project is largely complete. ☐
The project is very complete. ☐

❼ Sian is a fairly brilliant swimmer. ☐
Sian is an utterly brilliant swimmer. ☐

17.3 RESPOND OUT LOUD TO THE AUDIO, FILLING IN THE GAPS USING THE WORDS IN THE PANEL

Where are most of our products sold?

Our customer base is _____*largely*_____ Chinese.

1 Are you certain you sent the report?

_____ certain. I think I sent it yesterday.

2 Our new product range is really good!

Yeah, it's absolutely _____ . I love it.

3 Did you like Claude's presentation?

It was very impressive, but _____ identical to mine!

4 I've never seen a watch like yours before!

Yes, it's totally _____ . I have the only one.

5 Our new manager seems very popular.

That's right. _____ everyone likes him.

6 Did you enjoy the movie?

No. It was _____ awful. I almost fell asleep.

7 How was the event?

It was practically _____ . There were only a few people there.

fantastic   Nearly   almost   ~~largely~~   unique   absolutely   empty   Fairly

17.4 LISTEN TO THE AUDIO AND ANSWER THE QUESTIONS

Huong, the manager of a clothing brand, is being interviewed by Philippa, a journalist.

The employees at Huong's company are...
- fairly confident. ☐
- pretty happy. ☑
- completely miserable. ☐

1 Philippa thought the press release was...
- absolutely fantastic. ☐
- fairly interesting. ☐
- totally ridiculous. ☐

2 Philippa says that Huong's idea is...
- utterly ordinary. ☐
- largely unoriginal. ☐
- utterly original. ☐

3 Huong says that jogging during the day is...
- almost impossible. ☐
- always possible. ☐
- absolutely plausible. ☐

4 Huong says that during the day, people are...
- very busy. ☐
- absolutely exhausted. ☐
- extremely bored. ☐

5 According to Huong, exercise is...
- utterly essential. ☐
- pretty important. ☐
- extremely important. ☐

6 Huong developed a line that was...
- very expensive. ☐
- totally organic. ☐
- completely new. ☐

7 The stickers on the "NightJogging" line are...
- highly reflective. ☐
- wholly metallic. ☐
- pretty unusual. ☐

8 To begin with, promoting the line was...
- pretty difficult. ☐
- practically impossible. ☐
- extremely easy. ☐

9 Since a sports star offered support, it has been...
- absolutely amazing. ☐
- absolutely exhausting. ☐
- completely perfect. ☐

10 Philippa thinks the idea is...
- pretty confusing. ☐
- really complicated. ☐
- really clever. ☐

11 Huong thinks that launching in China is...
- thoroughly impractical. ☐
- fairly certain. ☐
- extremely unlikely. ☐

Advertising and branding

When you want to tell people about your company, product, or brand, intensifiers like "enough," "too," "so," and "such" can help communicate your point.

⚙ **New language** Intensifiers
Aa **Vocabulary** "Enough," "too," "so," and "such"
🧩 **New skill** Adding emphasis to descriptions

 18.1 LISTEN TO THE AUDIO AND MARK WHICH THINGS ARE DESCRIBED

 18.2 FILL IN THE GAPS WITH "SO" OR "SUCH"

 I work with ___such___ interesting people.

③ We've had _____ a fantastic year.

① There was _____ a large crowd outside.

④ The price for the hotel was _____ high.

② The results were _____ disappointing.

⑤ The week seems to pass _____ slowly.

65

18.3 REWRITE THE SENTENCES, PUTTING THE WORDS IN THE CORRECT ORDER

long | It | such | was | meeting. | a

It was such a long meeting.

1 so | coffee | expensive. | This | was

_____

2 is | My | colleague | lazy. | so

_____

3 so | Clara's | was | interesting. | presentation

_____

4 depressing | such | That | a | book. | is

_____

5 The | so | sales | disappointing. | were

_____

6 such | It's | a | story. | strange

_____

7 on | It's | to | important | time. | so | be

_____

18.4 READ THE ARTICLE AND ANSWER THE QUESTIONS

The ad is for an athletics club.
True ☐ **False** ✓ **Not given** ☐

1 Gym members receive a free T-shirt.
True ☐ **False** ☐ **Not given** ☐

2 Most adults think they don't get enough exercise.
True ☐ **False** ☐ **Not given** ☐

3 The gym offers a flexible timetable.
True ☐ **False** ☐ **Not given** ☐

4 Most people think they don't swim well enough.
True ☐ **False** ☐ **Not given** ☐

5 The gym offers swimming lessons for children.
True ☐ **False** ☐ **Not given** ☐

WELLNESS AND LIFESTYLE

Fellingdon Health & Sport

Feeling tired? Feeling low? Summer is here, and it's time for you to get fit, get healthy, and feel totally amazing with a free one-day pass to our gym and swimming pool in central Fellingdon.

In a recent survey 75 percent of adults said that they either don't get enough exercise, are too busy, or think that a gym would be too expensive. But our gym is affordable, and our timetable is flexible enough to fit the busiest schedule. And for those 23 percent of people who think they don't swim well enough, we offer training and expert advice. Get in touch now for a free quote!

18.5 CROSS OUT THE INCORRECT WORD IN EACH SENTENCE, THEN SAY THE SENTENCES OUT LOUD

I'd never seen ~~so~~ / such a big number of customers in the store before.

1. Our senior managers think the price of our products is **enough** / **too** high.

2. This room won't be big **enough** / **too** for this afternoon's meeting.

3. The team is **such** / **so** excited about tonight's awards ceremony.

4. I thought today's meeting was **such** / **so** a waste of time.

5. Jim doesn't speak loudly **enough** / **too**. I can barely hear him.

6. Our IT system is **enough** / **so** old. It's time we invested in a new one.

7. The new intern works **so** / **such** slowly. She prefers talking on the phone.

8. Our products were **so** / **too** expensive to appeal to middle-market customers.

9. Mary is **such** / **so** an ambitious woman. She wants to be a CEO by the age of 30.

10. You shouldn't drive **enough** / **too** quickly when you're in this part of town.

11. The strikes have caused **such** / **enough** a problem for our employees who commute.

12. The marketing campaign was **so** / **too** boring to appeal to young people.

19 Advice and suggestions

English uses modal verbs such as "could," "should," and "must" for advice or suggestions. They can be used to help co-workers in difficult or stressful situations.

⚙ **New language** Modal verbs for advice
Aa Vocabulary Workplace pressures
🧩 **New skill** Giving advice

19.1 MATCH THE SITUATIONS TO THE CORRECT ADVICE

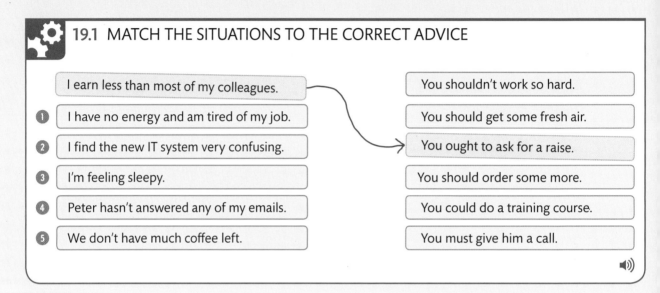

I earn less than most of my colleagues. ——→ You ought to ask for a raise.

You shouldn't work so hard.

1 I have no energy and am tired of my job.

You should get some fresh air.

2 I find the new IT system very confusing.

3 I'm feeling sleepy.

You should order some more.

4 Peter hasn't answered any of my emails.

You could do a training course.

5 We don't have much coffee left.

You must give him a call.

19.2 CROSS OUT THE INCORRECT WORDS IN EACH SENTENCE

You really **shouldn't** / ~~ought~~ eat your lunch in front of your computer.

1 You **could** / **shouldn't** try delegating the task to your team. I'm sure they'd do a great job.

2 Greg **ought to** / **ought** apologize to his team for his behavior. He was very rude.

3 Antonio really **ought to** / **shouldn't** employ some new staff, or we'll never meet our deadline.

4 We **should** / **should to** organize a training course for the interns.

5 The secretary really **should** / **couldn't** ask her boss for a raise. She works very hard.

19.3 FILL IN THE GAPS USING THE PHRASES IN THE PANEL

Cath ___*should move*___ if she lives too far from the office.

1 You _____ to work if the train is canceled.

2 You _____ the IT desk about your new password.

3 You _____ your lunch at your desk. Go to a café instead.

4 You _____ your manager when you want to book time off.

5 Clare _____ a break if she's tired of her job.

6 You _____ an English course if you want to learn English.

7 Dave _____ home if he's not feeling well.

8 Pete _____ to the public about company secrets.

could do
must tell
~~should move~~
ought to call
shouldn't eat
ought to go
shouldn't talk
should walk
ought to take

19.4 READ THE EMAIL AND MARK THE CORRECT SUMMARY

1 Vikram strongly advises Clara to make a list of her most important tasks. He suggests she might take a break from work for a week. ☐

2 Vikram says Clara must delegate her tasks to her team, and suggests she might ask another manager to help her complete her work. ☐

3 Vikram strongly advises Clara to list all her duties, and suggests she might ask a team member to complete half her work. ☐

4 Vikram strongly advises Clara to make a list of all her tasks, and suggests that she might ask her clients for more time. ☐

To: Clara McMillan

Subject: Re: Workload

Hi Clara,

Thanks for your email. I hope you're not finding the new position too stressful. Here's some advice that should help you to deal with your workload.

Firstly, you must make a list of all your duties and tasks, so you have a clear idea of what you have to do. You shouldn't try to do everything yourself.

You could definitely delegate more work to your team. I also think you ought to ask the client for more time to finish the project.

Remember that you shouldn't worry too much! This situation is quite typical for new employees here.

Best regards,
Vikram

19.5 REWRITE THE SENTENCES, CORRECTING THE ERRORS

> What about work at home on Friday?
> *What about working at home on Friday?*

1 Why don't we organizing a feedback session?

_____

2 What about ask Pedro to do it?

_____

3 Why don't you hiring some new staff?

_____

4 What about buy a new printer?

_____

5 Why doesn't Mabel going on vacation?

_____

6 Why not they close the Mumbai branch?

_____

7 What about invite the clients to dinner?

_____

🔊

19.6 LISTEN TO THE AUDIO AND MATCH THE IMAGES TO THE CORRECT PHRASES

19.7 USE THE CHART TO CREATE SIX CORRECT SENTENCES AND SAY THEM OUT LOUD

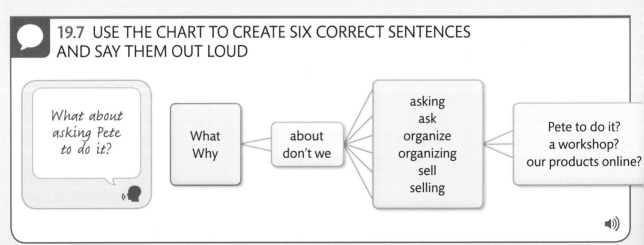

19.8 MARK THE SENTENCES THAT ARE CORRECT

Why don't we print out the data? ☑
Why don't we printing out the data? ☐

❹ Why don't we hiring a new secretary? ☐
Why don't we hire a new secretary? ☐

❶ What about organize a workshop? ☐
What about organizing a workshop? ☐

❺ What about asking Cyril to help? ☐
What about we asking Cyril to help? ☐

❷ Why don't we arrange a meeting? ☐
Why don't we arranging a meeting? ☐

❻ What about provide free software? ☐
What about providing free software? ☐

❸ What about we buying a new printer? ☐
What about buying a new printer? ☐

❼ Why don't we book a meeting room? ☐
Why we don't book a meeting room? ☐

🔊

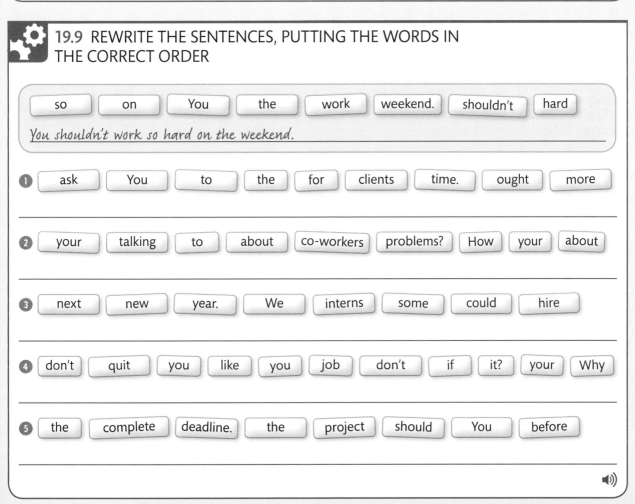

19.9 REWRITE THE SENTENCES, PUTTING THE WORDS IN THE CORRECT ORDER

| so | on | You | the | work | weekend. | shouldn't | hard |

You shouldn't work so hard on the weekend.

❶ | ask | You | to | the | for | clients | time. | ought | more |

_____

❷ | your | talking | to | about | co-workers | problems? | How | your | about |

_____

❸ | next | new | year. | We | interns | some | could | hire |

_____

❹ | don't | quit | you | like | you | job | don't | if | it? | your | Why |

_____

❺ | the | complete | deadline. | the | project | should | You | before |

_____

🔊

71

20 Vocabulary

Aa 20.1 MANAGEMENT AND LEADERSHIP WRITE THE PHRASES FROM THE PANEL UNDER THE CORRECT DEFINITIONS

To give a task to somebody

to allocate a task

1 Money added to a person's wages as a reward for good performance

_____

4 To give work or tasks to a person in a position junior to you

_____

5 How well a person carries out tasks

_____

Aa 20.2 SKILLS AND ABILITIES WRITE THE PHRASES FROM THE PANEL UNDER THE CORRECT PICTURES

initiative

1 _____

2 _____

3 _____

6 _____

7 _____

8 _____

9 _____

12 _____

13 _____

14 _____

15 _____

2 An interview to discuss an employee's performance

_____

3 To officially confirm something meets the required standards

_____

6 To be given a more senior position within a company

_____

to delegate   to approve   to be promoted

an appraisal / a performance review

performance   a bonus   ~~to allocate a task~~

---

4 _____

5 _____

10 _____

11 _____

16 _____

17 _____

IT / computing   written communication

data analysis   research   able to drive

fast learner   ~~initiative~~   teamwork

work well under pressure   organization

decision-making   numeracy

public speaking   problem-solving

leadership   telephone manner

attention to detail   time management

21 Talking about abilities

To talk about people's skills, for example in a performance review, you can use various modal verbs to express present, past, and future ability.

⚙ **New language** Modal verbs for abilities
Aa Vocabulary Workplace skills
🧩 **New skill** Describing abilities

⚙ 21.1 FILL IN THE GAPS USING "CAN" OR "CAN'T"

Jenny has great people skills. She _____ can _____ talk to all sorts of people.

1 Tom _____ fix your car this afternoon. It will be ready at 5:00.

2 Karl _____ drive. He failed his driving test again.

3 Jon used to be really nervous, but now he _____ give presentations.

4 She _____ type really quickly. She types over 60 words per minute.

5 I _____ work the new photocopier. It's too difficult.

6 Hansa is a really good cook. She _____ cook really nice Indian food.

7 Ali _____ read my handwriting. He says it's really messy.

8 Ania _____ speak French. She learned it in college.

9 Petra _____ manage her staff any more. They do what they like.

10 Parvesh _____ write clear reports. They are easy to read.

🔊

21.2 LISTEN TO THE AUDIO AND MARK WHETHER EACH PICTURE SHOWS PRESENT OR PAST ABILITY

Present ✓
Past ☐

① Present ☐
Past ☐

② Present ☐
Past ☐

③ Present ☐
Past ☐

④ Present ☐
Past ☐

21.3 REWRITE THE SENTENCES, CORRECTING THE ERRORS

George can't understand the old CEO because she had a strong accent.
George couldn't understand the old CEO because she had a strong accent.

① Janice can tell me if sales are up until she gets the final reports in.

_____

② Phil loves meeting new people, so he can't work in the HR department.

_____

③ Saira can't type fast, but now she can type 60 words a minute.

_____

④ Ed can't write reports very well. I'm going to ask him to help me write mine.

_____

⑤ Keira could use the database, but now she trains people in how to use it.

_____

⑥ For years Alex can't speak Arabic, but now he has done a beginners' course.

_____

🔊

21.4 READ THE PERFORMANCE REVIEW AND ANSWER THE QUESTIONS

Matt has worked for Pietro's for four years and has made good progress in that time. He joined us as an assistant chef and was rather unconfident in his cooking abilities then.

He didn't feel he could reach the standards required of a professional kitchen, but soon showed he was a very competent chef.

He was promoted two years ago to the position of head chef after proving he can create interesting and exciting menus with new dishes. His manager and I think he could be an excellent trainer of young chefs. We believe he would make a great mentor to talented young chefs.

Matt has worked at Pietro's for five years.
True ☐ False ☐ Not given ☑

① Matt has made little progress in his time at Pietro's.
True ☐ False ☐ Not given ☐

② He was a confident assistant chef.
True ☐ False ☐ Not given ☐

③ He particularly enjoys cooking Italian food.
True ☐ False ☐ Not given ☐

④ Matt has worked as head chef for four years.
True ☐ False ☐ Not given ☐

⑤ He can create exciting menus.
True ☐ False ☐ Not given ☐

⑥ He could be an excellent trainer of young chefs.
True ☐ False ☐ Not given ☐

21.5 MATCH THE PAIRS OF SENTENCES

Carrie is a great team member. — She would work well in any team.

① Jim is quite shy.　　　She could train staff to do them.

② Clare couldn't manage her old team.　　　He could be head of the department.

③ Carl is more confident now.　　　She can manage her new team much better.

④ Bea is good at giving presentations.　　　She wouldn't be a good trainer.

⑤ Jola is very impatient.　　　Before, he wouldn't talk in public.

⑥ Sam is very talented.　　　He would do well in a smaller team.

21.6 MARK THE SENTENCES THAT ARE CORRECT

> You're an excellent team member and you would do well on the sales team. ☑
> You're an excellent team member and you can't do well on the sales team. ☐

① David has given his team excellent training. Now they can't do anything. ☐
David has given his team excellent training. Now they can do anything. ☐

② Have you seen his brilliant designs? He can create our banners. ☐
Have you seen his brilliant designs? He couldn't create our banners. ☐

③ No one couldn't read the boss's handwriting. It was terrible. ☐
No one could read the boss's handwriting. It was terrible. ☐

④ Sebastian is a very proactive person and would do well in marketing. ☐
Sebastian is a very proactive person and couldn't do well in marketing. ☐

🔊

21.7 CROSS OUT THE INCORRECT WORD IN EACH SENTENCE, THEN SAY THE SENTENCES OUT LOUD

> If Jorge keeps on working hard, he ~~would~~ / **could** be area manager one day.

① We think you are very talented and **would** / **couldn't** be a great addition to our department.

② I don't know what is wrong with the coffee machine. I **can** / **can't** get it working.

③ My confidence is much better now. Before, I **couldn't** / **could** give presentations.

④ Laila couldn't negotiate with her old boss, but she **can't** / **can** with her new boss.

🔊

22 Comparing and contrasting

In team discussions, discourse markers can ease the flow of conversation. They can help link similar or contrasting ideas, or connect an action to a result.

⚙ **New language** Discourse markers
Aa Vocabulary Teamwork and team building
🧩 **New skill** Expressing your ideas

22.1 CROSS OUT THE INCORRECT WORDS IN EACH SENTENCE

 Team A enjoyed the task a lot. Team B found it very rewarding **as well** / ~~however~~.

1. This training is really interesting. It is a lot of fun, **also** / **too**.

2. Team-building days are useful. They are **also** / **too** fun.

3. Some people always wash their coffee cups, **while** / **as well** others don't.

4. **However** / **Although** Team A did the task quickly, Team B didn't finish it.

5. Team A built the bridge very quickly. Team B was **as well** / **equally** successful.

6. Team A helped each other, **while** / **as well** Team B disagreed with each other.

7. Hard work is an excellent trait in a team, **equally** / **whereas** laziness is terrible.

8. Yesterday's training was useful. **However** / **Although**, this morning's task was pointless.

9. Some people want to lead a team, **as well** / **while** others are happy to be team members.

10. It is important to say what we all think. We should listen to each other **as well** / **equally**.

11. This training is very useful. It is **equally** / **as well** a good way to get to know people.

🔊

22.2 MARK THE SENTENCES THAT ARE CORRECT

> We learned a lot from that training session, whereas it was a lot of fun. ☐
> We learned a lot from that training session. It was a lot of fun, too. ☑

1. However, Sam went to the training day, he didn't learn anything new. ☐
   Although Sam went to the training day, he didn't learn anything new. ☐

2. Team A solved the problem really quickly. Team B was equally successful. ☐
   Team A solved the problem really quickly. Team B was as well successful. ☐

3. This training is useful for managers. It is too useful for team members. ☐
   This training is useful for managers. It is also useful for team members. ☐

4. Some people want to be managers, while others want to be team members. ☐
   Some people want to be managers, as well others want to be team members. ☐

5. Laziness is a terrible trait for a team member, whereas honesty is excellent. ☐
   Laziness is a terrible trait for a team member, also honesty is excellent. ☐

6. We'd like all staff to follow our usual dress code for the training. Please be on time, however. ☐
   We'd like all staff to follow our usual dress code for the training. Please be on time, too. ☐

22.3 LISTEN TO THE AUDIO, THEN NUMBER THE SENTENCES IN THE ORDER THAT YOU HEAR THEM

A team leader is giving feedback on her team's performance in a task.

A. Team A was the first to complete the task. ☐

B. This was a very challenging task. ☐ 1

C. Creative thinking can be equally useful. ☐

D. It is important to read instructions carefully. ☐

E. However, Team B worked well together, too. ☐

F. We hope you also found it very rewarding. ☐

22.4 REWRITE THE SENTENCES, PUTTING THE WORDS IN THE CORRECT ORDER

| people | in | Some | prefer | while | team, | others | working | enjoy | alone. | a | working |

Some people enjoy working in a team, while others prefer working alone.

① | was | The | and | it | useful | lot | task | also | of | was | team-building | fun. | a |

_____

② | to | pizza. | had | Team A | a | build | make | had | a | Team B | bridge, | whereas | to |

_____

③ | some | had | the | Team B | completed | While | task | problems. | first, | they |

_____

④ | often | as well. | really | they | are | courses | and | fun | are | Training | useful |

_____

⑤ | was | Team A | cooperative. | equally | together | Team B | worked | as | well. | very |

_____

⑥ | identify | This | your | task | weaknesses, | also | strengths. | will | your | but |

_____

⑦ | a | team | However, | didn't | cake. | the | activity | baked | matter. | Our |

_____

⑧ | worked | other | Although | we | came | first, | together. | the | team | well |

_____

⑨ | easy, | today's | Yesterday's | difficult. | more | task | was | task | was | while |

_____

⑩ | the | finished | its | took | Team A | whereas | task | time. | quickly, | Team B |

_____

🔊

22.5 MATCH THE PAIRS OF SENTENCES

The team worked well together.	Consequently, they all won a medal.
1 The course taught me how to manage people.	As a result, everyone attends them.
2 Team Orange completed the challenge first.	As a result, they completed the task.
3 I'd never driven a forklift truck before.	Consequently, she was promoted last week.
4 The training days are useful.	As a consequence, I am now a team leader.
5 Jess learned a lot from the training.	For this reason, I was very nervous.

22.6 SAY THE SENTENCES OUT LOUD, FILLING IN THE GAPS USING THE WORDS IN THE PANEL

The task taught us how to run a team. As a _____result_____ , I now lead a team of ten.

1 Team-building days are great for morale. _____ , the atmosphere in our office is good.

2 We have regular IT training sessions. For this _____ , everyone has good computer skills.

3 We do team building every year. As a _____ , we work really well together.

4 During team building we meet new staff. _____ reason, we know our co-workers well.

For this	consequence	Consequently	result	reason

23 Planning events

Many English verbs that are used to give opinions or talk about plans, intentions, and arrangements are followed by a gerund or an infinitive.

⚙ **New language** Verb patterns
Aa Vocabulary Corporate entertainment
New skill Talking about business events

 23.1 CROSS OUT THE INCORRECT WORDS IN EACH SENTENCE

We must keep ~~to remind~~ / **reminding** customers of our new product range.

❶ We plan **to launch** / **launching** our new product range at the conference.

❷ Would you consider **to organize** / **organizing** the accommodation for the visitors?

❸ I really enjoy **to take** / **taking** clients out for dinner at famous restaurants.

❹ Jenny has offered **to meet** / **meeting** our visitors at the airport.

❺ I keep **to suggest** / **suggesting** that we should have a staff training session.

🔊

 23.2 REWRITE THE SENTENCES, CORRECTING THE ERRORS

I really enjoy to give presentations.
I really enjoy giving presentations.

❶ Our clients expect receive good customer service.

❷ Would you consider to make the name badges for the delegates?

❸ Colin has offered organizing the training program for the new staff.

❹ I hope impressing our clients when I show them around the new office.

🔊

CORPORATE EVENTS

RED GIRAFFE EVENTS PLANNING

How we can plan the ideal event for your company

Red Giraffe is an international events management business. We are one of the biggest events organizers in the US, and our clients range from start-up businesses to large corporations. We enjoy all aspects of the job, but the most enjoyable is entertaining clients. Our clients expect to receive excellent service and we pride ourselves on meeting their every requirement. We often take clients out for lunch during the planning phase to talk about their requirements. It's good to do this over a meal as they say what they really want when they are relaxed and enjoying the food.

Kayaking is one of the team-building events that Red Giraffe will offer soon.

After lunch, we have a brainstorming session in groups. When all the clients have arrived, we serve coffee as it helps to get the ideas flowing. All kinds of things come up in these sessions. For instance, when we planned a launch for a media company, the employees kept saying we should have a boat trip on the river. But some people didn't like this idea because their competitors had done the same, so we went for a covered venue in a converted warehouse. Next year, we plan to start offering team-building events, such as sports days and treasure hunts. We expect these to be very popular with our clients.

What clients does Red Giraffe work with?

Small start-up businesses ☐
Only big corporate clients ☐
All sizes of business ☑

① What do the company's employees enjoy?

Entertaining clients ☐
Organizing refreshments ☐
Having great accommodation ☐

② What do the company's clients expect?

To have a free lunch ☐
To receive good customer service ☐
To eat a planned dinner ☐

③ Why should you go out for a meal with clients?

They like eating great food ☐
They like talking about the food ☐
They give their honest opinion ☐

④ Why didn't one client want to have a boat trip?

They wanted an outdoor venue ☐
Their competitors had had one ☐
Their CEO didn't like boats ☐

⑤ What does Red Giraffe plan to do next year?

Offer team-building events ☐
Go on a treasure hunt ☐
Become popular with clients ☐

23.4 FILL IN THE GAPS USING THE WORDS IN THE PANEL

Did you remember _____*to call*_____ the hotel about the catering?

1 I regret _____ you that I can't take the clients out for dinner. I'm very sorry.

2 Do you remember _____ Dan last month? He has a question about a discount you offered.

3 Sue stopped _____ the program for the launch event. It looked really interesting!

4 He regrets _____ her his idea for the event because she copied it.

5 David gave his presentation, and went on _____ about new events.

6 I stopped _____ my presentation because the CEO had a question.

| to talk | giving | telling | calling | to read | ~~to call~~ | to tell |

🔊

23.5 LISTEN TO THE AUDIO, THEN NUMBER THE PICTURES IN THE ORDER THEY ARE DESCRIBED

A ☐

B ☐ 1

C ☐

8:30 WESTFORD

D ☐

E ☐

F ☐

G ☐

H ☐

23.6 REWRITE THE SENTENCES, PUTTING THE WORDS IN THE CORRECT ORDER

| visitors | at | has | the | to | our | offered | airport. | Kelly | meet |

Kelly has offered to meet our visitors at the airport.

① | entertaining | I | clients. | enjoy | really | new |

_____

② | invited | the | Sandra | overseas | to | conference. | me | sales | attend |

_____

③ | book | My | the | asked | to | accommodation. | manager | me |

_____

④ | him | Tom | manager | a | soon. | expects | promotion | his | to | give |

_____

⑤ | me | recent | My | to | give | sales. | him | asked | an | on | boss | update |

_____

⑥ | our | come | We | to | all | to | party. | invited | customers | our |

_____

🔊

23.7 USE THE CHART TO CREATE 16 CORRECT SENTENCES AND SAY THEM OUT LOUD

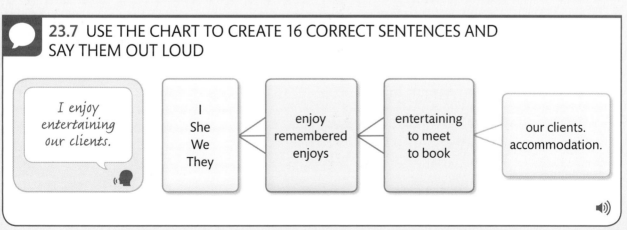

🔊

85

24 Vocabulary

To conclude

to sum up

1 To write a record of what
was said during a meeting

3 To answer questions

4 To be not present

6 To have no more time left
to do something

7 A plan for achieving
a particular goal

9 Proposals for specific action
to be taken

10 To present information
to a group of people

12 To say something before
someone else has finished speaking

13 People who have been to
or are going to a meeting

15 When everyone agrees

16 To look again at the written record
of a past meeting

2 To consider or focus on something

---

5 To come to an agreement about an issue

---

8 The primary aim

---

11 To send a plan for what will be discussed

---

14 To put forward an idea or plan for others to discuss

---

17 A vote made by raising hands in the air to show agreement

---

a show of hands   attendees

action points   to give a presentation

to take minutes   to suggest / propose

to send out an agenda   to look at

~~to sum up~~   to review the minutes

main objective   to interrupt

to be absent   unanimous agreement

a strategy   to reach a consensus

to run out of time   to take questions

25 What people said

When telling co-workers what someone else said, you can take what they said (direct speech) and rephrase it accurately and clearly. This is called reported speech.

⚙ **New language** Reported speech
Aa Vocabulary Meetings
🧩 **New skill** Reporting what someone said

25.1 MATCH THE DIRECT SPEECH TO THE REPORTED SPEECH

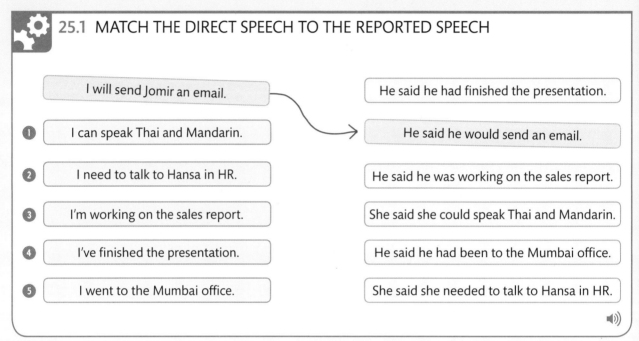

I will send Jomir an email. → He said he would send an email.

He said he had finished the presentation.

1 I can speak Thai and Mandarin.

2 I need to talk to Hansa in HR.

3 I'm working on the sales report.

4 I've finished the presentation.

5 I went to the Mumbai office.

He said he was working on the sales report.

She said she could speak Thai and Mandarin.

He said he had been to the Mumbai office.

She said she needed to talk to Hansa in HR.

25.2 REWRITE THE SENTENCES AS REPORTED SPEECH USING "SAID"

I met Jo from HR.
She _said she had met Jo from HR._

3 I will get the bill.
He _____

1 The taxi is outside.
She _____

4 I can't open any emails.
He _____

2 I need to call the US office.
He _____

5 I have sent the order to them.
She _____

25.3 REWRITE THE SENTENCES, PUTTING THE WORDS IN THE CORRECT ORDER

| said | He | figures! | couldn't | those | believe | he |

He said he couldn't believe those figures!

---

1 | busy | she | that | was | She | afternoon. | said |

---

2 | his | like | He | that | he | didn't | boss. | said | new |

---

3 | received | said | hadn't | the | they | delivery. | They |

---

4 | was | He | to | in | week. | Tokyo | that | going | said | be | he |

---

5 | to | new | had | product | They | been | the | said | launch. | they |

---

6 | invoice | She | away. | right | would | she | an | said | issue |

---

7 | give | company | said | 5 percent | the | could | discount. | a | He |

---

8 | said | she | the | had | well | gotten | interviewer. | along | She | with |

---

9 | said | They | were | they | range. | a | new | designing |

25.4 LISTEN TO THE AUDIO, THEN NUMBER THE REPORTED SENTENCES IN THE ORDER YOU HEAR THEM AS DIRECT SPEECH

Suzanne is talking to a co-worker throughout the day.

A Suzanne said she'd send him the report the following day. ☐

B Suzanne said she had met the new CEO in the Miami office that week. 1

C Suzanne said her laptop wasn't working that day. ☐

D Suzanne said she could help Alemay prepare her presentation that afternoon. ☐

E Suzanne said she had come into work early that morning. ☐

F Suzanne said she had to stay late and call the Mexico office that evening. ☐

G Suzanne said she was going to design a new app with Tim the week after. ☐

25.5 CROSS OUT THE INCORRECT WORDS IN EACH SENTENCE

Jake ~~told~~ / said that he wanted a promotion before the end of the year.

1 He said / told me that he'd been to China twice.

2 She suggested / said that she was going to Montreal.

3 He promised / told that he wouldn't be late for the train.

4 He explained / promised that he didn't know how to use the photocopier.

5 He denied / told that he had broken the coffee machine.

6 She promised / complained that the food was cold when the waiter brought it.

7 He confirmed / announced that the tickets had been booked.

🔊

25.6 REPORT THE DIRECT SPEECH IN THE AUDIO OUT LOUD, FILLING IN THE GAPS USING THE WORDS IN THE PANEL

I am not the person in charge of this project.

He _____ denied _____ that he was the person in charge of that project.

1. I'll definitely call you back after 2:30 this afternoon.

She _____ to call me back after 2:30 that afternoon.

2. I need a printout, and I will also need a copy of Simon's report about the year-end accounts.

He _____ that he needed a copy of Simon's report about the year-end accounts.

3. The new all-in-one printer isn't difficult to use.

She _____ that the new all-in-one printer wasn't difficult to use.

4. Yes, that's right. I'd like to buy 100 units of the new product.

He _____ that he'd like to buy 100 units of the new product.

5. I'm not happy with the customer service I have experienced.

He _____ that he wasn't happy with the customer service he had experienced.

6. How about asking Ameera what she thinks?

She _____ that we should ask Ameera what she thought.

explained   promised   suggested   complained   added   ~~denied~~   confirmed

91

What people asked

You can use reported questions to tell someone what someone else has asked. Direct questions and reported questions have different word orders.

New language Reported questions
Aa Vocabulary "Have," "make," "get," "do"
New skill Reporting what someone asked

26.1 REWRITE THE SENTENCES, PUTTING THE WORDS IN THE CORRECT ORDER

| how | Kevin | gone. | asked | negotiations | me | the | had |

Kevin asked me how the negotiations had gone.

1 | where | Selma | put | me | you | annual | the | report. | asked | had |

_____

2 | wanted | Krishnan | why | was | know | I | late | again. | to | for | work |

_____

3 | asked | My | what | I | the | IT | new | about | me | system. | boss | thought |

_____

4 | me | asked | Hans | would | where | we | have | the | afternoon. | presentation | this |

_____

5 | wasn't | he | Sophie | Claude | why | at | meeting. | asked | the |

_____

6 | me | Tabitha | who | cell | taken | her | phone. | asked | had |

_____

7 | the | Fiona | to | had | know | who | minutes. | wanted | taken |

_____

Sam is telling Shelly about a conversation that he had with Doug.

Doug is feeling confident about the conference.
True ☐ **False** ☑ **Not given** ☐

❶ Shelly has booked the flights for Monday.
True ☐ **False** ☐ **Not given** ☐

❷ The Hotel Belle Vue is fully booked.
True ☐ **False** ☐ **Not given** ☐

❸ Shelly has booked the rooms for three nights.
True ☐ **False** ☐ **Not given** ☐

❹ The Classic Inn includes breakfast.
True ☐ **False** ☐ **Not given** ☐

❺ There are meeting facilities at the Classic Inn.
True ☐ **False** ☐ **Not given** ☐

❻ Doug is planning to bring his family.
True ☐ **False** ☐ **Not given** ☐

❼ Shelly has finished the promotional materials.
True ☐ **False** ☐ **Not given** ☐

❽ Shelly also has to prepare a presentation.
True ☐ **False** ☐ **Not given** ☐

❾ Ted can help Shelly with her work.
True ☐ **False** ☐ **Not given** ☐

Aa 26.3 MATCH THE DEFINITIONS TO THE COLLOCATIONS

explain to someone what they have done wrong → have a word

❶ offer advice or ideas

❷ lose your job because of misconduct

❸ misunderstand, or do something incorrectly

❹ try as hard as you can

❺ help someone without thought of reward

❻ find work

❼ investigate a topic, or discover information

❽ write down information during a meeting

make a suggestion

make a mistake

have a word

get fired

do someone a favor

make notes

do research

do your best

get a job

26.4 REWRITE THE SENTENCES, TURNING THEM INTO REPORTED QUESTIONS

Who took the minutes yesterday?
She *asked me who had taken the minutes yesterday.*

1 How many people work in the company?

She _____

2 Why did you hand in the report so late?

He _____

3 Who got promoted?

He _____

4 Who is the new senior manager?

He _____

5 Which candidate did you choose?

She _____

6 How long have you worked here?

He _____

7 Why were you so late this morning?

She _____

8 What time do you get home?

He _____

9 Where did you have the appointment?

He _____

10 Which printer do you prefer?

She _____

26.5 SAY THE DIRECT QUESTIONS OUT LOUD, TURNING THEM INTO REPORTED QUESTIONS

Did you make notes during the meeting?

He _____asked me if I had made notes during the meeting._____ .

1 Did the package arrive safely?

He _____ .

2 Can you do me a favor?

She _____ .

3 Can I have a word with you later?

He _____ .

4 Have you finished writing the report yet?

She _____ .

5 Can I make a suggestion?

He _____ .

6 Did you read last year's report?

She _____ .

7 Are you coming to the awards ceremony on Saturday?

He _____ .

8 Did you enjoy the presentation?

She _____ .

9 Have you booked a table at the restaurant?

He _____ .

27 Reporting quantities

In presentations and reports, you may need to talk about how much of something there is. The words you can use to do this depend on the thing you are describing.

⚙ **New language** "Few," "little," and "all"
Aa Vocabulary Meetings
🧩 **New skill** Talking about quantity

 27.1 READ THE REPORT AND ANSWER THE QUESTIONS

Sales have grown fast in the last year.
True ☐ **False** ☑ **Not given** ☐

1 China has been a strong competitor over the last year.
True ☐ **False** ☐ **Not given** ☐

2 There is not much chance of a quick solution.
True ☐ **False** ☐ **Not given** ☐

3 The company should reduce its prices dramatically.
True ☐ **False** ☐ **Not given** ☐

4 The most expensive product made in China costs $25.
True ☐ **False** ☐ **Not given** ☐

5 The brand is well known among older people.
True ☐ **False** ☐ **Not given** ☐

6 The brand is unpopular with teenagers.
True ☐ **False** ☐ **Not given** ☐

7 The company's advertising campaign is old.
True ☐ **False** ☐ **Not given** ☐

8 The company needs to open more stores in Asia.
True ☐ **False** ☐ **Not given** ☐

9 It costs less to open stores in Asia than Europe.
True ☐ **False** ☐ **Not given** ☐

10 Asia is not a very valuable market for the company.
True ☐ **False** ☐ **Not given** ☐

REPORT

Problem:
Over the past 12 months, our overseas sales have fallen dramatically. Competition from Asia, particularly China, is intense.

Proposed solutions:
There is little we can do to turn this situation around in the next couple of months. However, if we take a long-term view, there are a few solutions.

1) We can lower our prices a little. This will make our products more price-competitive. Currently, our products are 15–25% more expensive than China-made products.

2) We can launch a new advertising campaign. Our research suggests that few people over the age of 50 have heard of our brand. This is a big market we can access if we get our advertising message right. At the other end of the market, very few teenagers seem interested in our products. We need to position our advertising to make our brand appear current and fashionable.

3) We have very few stores in Asia. We can consider opening a few more stores in Asia so that we can become a more familiar brand in this important market.

27.2 MARK THE SENTENCES THAT ARE CORRECT

There's little bit of money left in the budget to redesign the website. ☐
There's a little bit of money left in the budget to redesign the website. ☑

1 Unfortunately, we have few problems with our production line. ☐
Unfortunately, we have a few problems with our production line. ☐

2 Regrettably, few people have the skills necessary to run a multinational company. ☐
Regrettably, a few people have the skills necessary to run a multinational company. ☐

3 So few of our customer reviews are positive that it's becoming a problem. ☐
So a few of our customer reviews are positive that it's becoming a problem. ☐

4 I have a little doubt that the conference will be a success. ☐
I have little doubt that the conference will be a success. ☐

27.3 CROSS OUT THE INCORRECT WORDS IN EACH SENTENCE, THEN SAY THE SENTENCES OUT LOUD

We have very **few** / ~~little~~ rooms left on the 12th of December.

1 **A little** / **Few** employees have worked for the company for as long as Sofia.

2 We have **little** / **a little** bit of time before the meeting ends.

3 So **few** / **a few** companies offer this service that demand is sure to be high.

4 Very **few** / **little** can be done to improve facilities in the short term.

5 We can expect **a few** / **a little** increase in profits over the summer season.

6 It's great that you have **few** / **a few** ideas about how we can improve sales.

27.4 REWRITE THE SENTENCES, PUTTING THE WORDS IN THE CORRECT ORDER

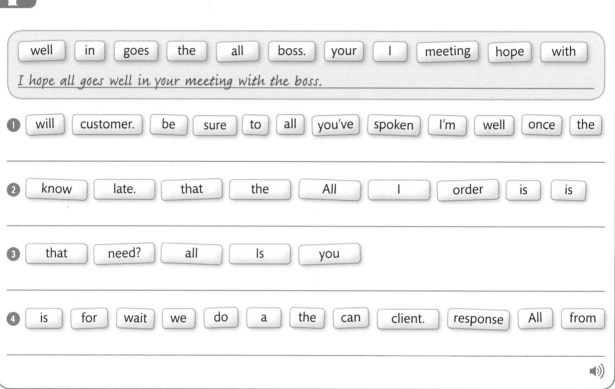

well   in   goes   the   all   boss.   your   I   meeting   hope   with

I hope all goes well in your meeting with the boss.

1 will   customer.   be   sure   to   all   you've   spoken   I'm   well   once   the

_____

2 know   late.   that   the   All   I   order   is   is

_____

3 that   need?   all   Is   you

_____

4 is   for   wait   we   do   a   the   can   client.   response   All   from

_____

27.5 MATCH THE PAIRS OF SENTENCES THAT MEAN THE SAME THING

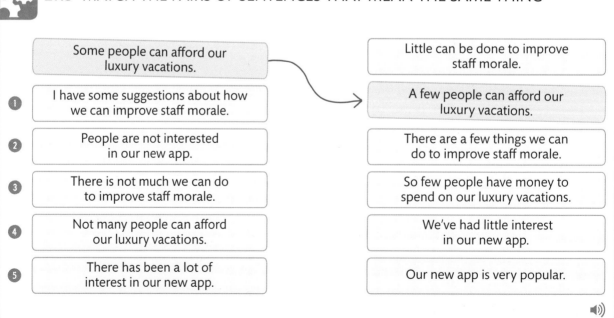

Some people can afford our luxury vacations.

Little can be done to improve staff morale.

1 I have some suggestions about how we can improve staff morale.

A few people can afford our luxury vacations.

2 People are not interested in our new app.

There are a few things we can do to improve staff morale.

3 There is not much we can do to improve staff morale.

So few people have money to spend on our luxury vacations.

4 Not many people can afford our luxury vacations.

We've had little interest in our new app.

5 There has been a lot of interest in our new app.

Our new app is very popular.

28 Checking information

Sometimes you may need to clarify whether you have understood a point. There are a number of ways to politely check information in conversation.

✿ **New language** Subject questions, question tags
Aa Vocabulary Polite checks and echo questions
✦ **New skill** Checking information

28.1 REWRITE THE QUESTIONS, PUTTING THE WORDS IN THE CORRECT ORDER

| is | price? | the | What | sale |

What is the sale price?

❶ year? | is | target | our | this | What

_____

❷ account? | is | Who | the | handling

_____

❸ in | Who | is | charge?

_____

❹ your | target? | sales | is | What

_____

❺ complaints? | Who | to | responds

_____

❻ Jones? | Who | Mr. | spoke | to

_____

❼ action? | plan | is | What | our | of

_____

28.2 MARK THE BEST QUESTION FOR EACH REPLY

☑ Who made the most sales? / ☐ Did Yousef make the most sales?
— Yousef made the most sales.

❶ ☐ Do I need to dress formally? / ☐ What is the dress code?
— Yes, you do.

❷ ☐ Did you quote this price? / ☐ Who quoted this price?
— No, I didn't.

❸ ☐ What should I tell the client? / ☐ Should I tell the client the truth?
— You should tell them the truth.

❹ ☐ Does he want to work in New York? / ☐ Who wants to work in New York?
— Ian would love to work in New York.

28.3 MATCH THE BEGINNINGS OF THE SENTENCES TO THE CORRECT ENDINGS

Joel is our best negotiator, → isn't he?

am I?

did I?

isn't he?

1. We should increase our margins,

2. I didn't send you the report,

didn't he?

3. She'll be a great manager,

4. I'm not getting a raise,

aren't we?

5. We haven't made a loss,

shouldn't we?

6. We're going to win the award,

have we?

7. Louis has worked here since 2012,

won't she?

8. Brett worked late last night,

hasn't he?

28.4 FILL IN THE GAPS USING THE CORRECT QUESTION TAGS

I've made a mistake, _____*haven't I?*_____

1. We could launch our product early, _____

2. Jakob ordered the samples, _____

3. We can't cut prices any further, _____

4. We haven't achieved our target, _____

5. We need to improve product quality, _____

6. We're not ready for the meeting, _____

7. They are opening a new store, _____

8. You weren't in London last week, _____

9. You traveled to Paris by train, _____

10. I'm writing the proposal, _____

11. I emailed the right person, _____

28.5 LISTEN TO THE AUDIO AND ANSWER THE QUESTIONS

A sales assistant is calling his manager to check a few details and confirm information.

Anya is very busy when Mike calls.
True ☐ False ☐ Not given ☑

1 The conference takes place every year.
True ☐ False ☐ Not given ☐

2 Mike's plan is to put out 100 seats.
True ☐ False ☐ Not given ☐

3 Only five people have replied to the invitation.
True ☐ False ☐ Not given ☐

4 Anya thinks they should put out 140 seats.
True ☐ False ☐ Not given ☐

5 Pauline is dealing with the food and drink.
True ☐ False ☐ Not given ☐

6 Anya wants her guests to feel welcome.
True ☐ False ☐ Not given ☐

7 Anya will contact Francesca about catering.
True ☐ False ☐ Not given ☐

28.6 CROSS OUT THE INCORRECT WORDS IN EACH SENTENCE, THEN SAY THE SENTENCES OUT LOUD

They received government funding, didn't they / ~~did they~~?

1 What was her name? I didn't listen / hear it.

2 Who / What is responsible for training?

3 You're not worried about the meeting, aren't you / are you?

4 What / Who is our timetable for this project?

5 Sales are better than expected, aren't they / are they?

6 Sorry, I lost / missed that.

29 Vocabulary

Aa 29.1 INDUSTRIES WRITE THE WORDS FROM THE PANEL UNDER THE CORRECT PICTURES

shipping

1 _____

2 _____

3 _____

4 _____

5 _____

6 _____

7 _____

8 _____

9 _____

10 _____

11 _____

12 _____

13 _____

14 _____

15 _____

16 _____

17 _____

18 _____

19 _____

fashion   catering / food   tourism   recycling   transportation   hospitality   energy

manufacturing   finance   agriculture / farming   electronics   ~~shipping~~   chemical   healthcare

real estate (US) / property (UK)   fishing   education   pharmaceutical   mining   entertainment

Aa 29.2 PROFESSIONAL ATTRIBUTES WRITE THE WORDS FROM THE PANEL UNDER THE CORRECT PICTURES

flexible

1 _____

2 _____

3 _____

4 _____

5 _____

6 _____

7 _____

8 _____

9 _____

10 _____

11 _____

12 _____

13 _____

14 _____

15 _____

creative	reliable	practical	professional	~~flexible~~
motivated	confident	ambitious	accurate	team player
organized	energetic	responsible	punctual	innovative	calm

30 Job descriptions

English uses "a" or "an" in descriptions of jobs and to introduce new information. The zero article refers to general things, and "the" refers to specific things.

 New language Articles
Aa Vocabulary Job descriptions and applications
New skill Describing a job

30.1 CROSS OUT THE INCORRECT WORDS IN EACH SENTENCE

I applied for a job as ~~a~~/an / ~~the~~ IT engineer. ~~A~~ / ~~An~~ / The salary is really good.

① I want to apply for **a / an / the** job in **a / an / the** office.

② I've got **a / an / the** interview next week for **a / an / the** job I told you about.

③ **A / An / The** ideal candidate enjoys working in **a / an / the** team.

④ **A / An / The** deadline for applications for **a / an / the** job in IT is next Monday.

⑤ Please complete **a / an / the** form on **a / an / the** job page on our website.

30.2 LISTEN TO THE AUDIO, THEN NUMBER THE PICTURES IN THE ORDER THEY ARE DESCRIBED

 A ☐

 B 1

 C ☐

 D ☐

 E ☐

 F ☐

 G ☐

 H ☐

30.3 MARK THE SENTENCES THAT ARE CORRECT

> Mark loves teaching students. The students he teaches at the college are all adults. ☑
> Mark loves teaching the students. Students he teaches at the college are all adults. ☐

1 The nurses often have to work very long hours. They are the very important people. ☐
Nurses often have to work very long hours. They are very important people. ☐

2 Working hours are from 8:30 to 5:00. Lunch is from 1:00 to 2:00. ☐
The working hours are from 8:30 to 5:00. The lunch is from 1:00 to 2:00. ☐

3 Vale loves giving training sessions. The training sessions she gave yesterday were amazing. ☐
Vale loves giving the training sessions. Training sessions she gave yesterday were amazing. ☐

4 Job I applied for is based in Madrid. It's in the sales and marketing. ☐
The job I applied for is based in Madrid. It's in sales and marketing. ☐

5 The people who interviewed me for the job were really nice. They were managers. ☐
People who interviewed me for the job were really nice. They were the managers. ☐

6 I have just applied for a job in finance department at your company. ☐
I have just applied for a job in the finance department at your company. ☐

7 The salary for this job is not very good. I don't think I'll apply for it. ☐
Salary for this job is not very good. I don't think I'll apply for it. ☐

8 The successful candidate will have three years' experience branding new products. ☐
Successful candidate will have three years' experience branding the new products. ☐

9 Our company is currently recruiting more the staff for Paris office. ☐
Our company is currently recruiting more staff for the Paris office. ☐

10 I have the meetings with CEO and some of our new clients today. ☐
I have meetings with the CEO and some of our new clients today. ☐

11 Marisha is good at pitching products. It's the thing she enjoys most about her job. ☐
Marisha is good at pitching the products. It's thing she enjoys most about her job. ☐

12 This job requires in-depth knowledge of business trends in the wider world. ☐
This job requires the in-depth knowledge of the business trends in wider world. ☐

◀))

30.4 READ THE JOB DESCRIPTION AND ANSWER THE QUESTIONS

The job is a sales and marketing role.
True ✓ **False** ☐

1 No previous experience is needed.
True ☐ **False** ☐

2 The job involves giving presentations.
True ☐ **False** ☐

3 The job requires market-specific knowledge.
True ☐ **False** ☐

4 No leadership experience is needed.
True ☐ **False** ☐

5 The successful candidate will have training.
True ☐ **False** ☐

VACANCIES

Arctic Foods
Sales and Marketing Manager

Do you have a passion for selling new ideas? Then we could have the job for you.

Arctic Foods is looking for a dynamic sales and marketing manager. You will have previous experience in a sales and marketing role, preferably in the frozen food sector. You will be good at giving presentations and fully up to date with market trends. Previous experience leading a sizeable team is essential.

Full product training will be given to the successful candidate.

30.5 CROSS OUT THE INCORRECT WORDS IN EACH SENTENCE, THEN SAY THE SENTENCES OUT LOUD

At the second-round interview, you will meet ~~HR manager~~ / the HR manager.

1 We need someone who is willing to travel, and can speak the Spanish / Spanish.

2 Tara works in the finance department / finance department of an advertising agency.

3 Marc and Samantha often travel to China on business / on the business.

4 The company is based in the UK, but it does business throughout EU / the EU.

5 I started looking for a job as an engineer / the engineer after I finished college.

31 Applying for a job

Cover letters for job applications should sound fluent and confident. Using the correct prepositions after verbs, nouns, and adjectives can help you achieve this.

New language Dependent prepositions
Aa Vocabulary Cover-letter vocabulary
New skill Writing a cover letter

 31.1 MATCH THE PICTURES TO THE CORRECT SENTENCES

I am fully trained in all aspects of health and safety.

1

I have several years of experience in the catering industry.

2

I graduated from college in June 2016 with a degree in chemistry.

3

I am writing to apply for the role of head chef.

4

I heard about the job on your website.

31.2 CROSS OUT THE INCORRECT WORDS IN EACH SENTENCE

At college, I focused ~~in~~ / on / ~~at~~ business studies. It has been very useful in my career.

1 Jim graduated **from** / **at** / **out** college with a degree in physics. Now he is a research scientist.

2 He is fully trained **to** / **with** / **in** all aspects of sales and marketing. I think he'll do a great job.

3 In my role as Senior Program Developer, I reported **in** / **on** / **to** the Director of IT.

4 Tanya has applied **at** / **for** / **on** a job in the marketing department of our company.

5 I worked **at** / **of** / **for** the owner of a leading hairdressing salon. I learned a lot from him.

🔊

31.3 READ THE COVER LETTER AND WRITE ANSWERS TO THE QUESTIONS AS FULL SENTENCES

Why is Ellie writing the letter?

To apply for the role of Head of Marketing.

1 How long has Ellie worked in marketing?

_____

2 What did she develop in her previous jobs?

_____

3 What did she introduce last year?

_____

4 What is she responsible for in her current job?

_____

5 Which region does she look after?

_____

6 How does she describe herself?

_____

Dear Ms. Jenkins,

I am writing to apply for the position of Head of Marketing as advertised on your company website.

I have more than ten years' experience in marketing, and I have worked in the marketing departments of several big companies, where I developed award-winning campaigns in key markets. Last year I was responsible for introducing a new customer-focused branding initiative.

In my current position, I am responsible for training junior members of staff. I run the sales and marketing operations for the Europe region. This includes setting the sales and marketing strategy for the region.

I would welcome the opportunity to learn new skills. I am also energetic, dynamic, and extremely reliable.

Please find attached my résumé and references. I look forward to hearing from you.

Yours sincerely,

Ellie Abrahams

honest and trustworthy → a position

reliable

1. a set of abilities resulting from experience → reliable

2. a fixed regular payment — to report to someone

3. a job — skills

4. to make an official request for a job — salary

5. to have someone in charge of you — a team

6. the group of people you work with — a résumé

7. a document detailing your skills — an opportunity

8. a chance to do something — to amount to

9. to equal a total number — to apply for a job

🔊

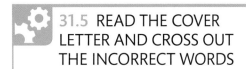

31.5 READ THE COVER LETTER AND CROSS OUT THE INCORRECT WORDS

3257 Gateway Drive
Portland, OR
March 29, 2014

Dear Mr. Chang,

I am writing to ~~apply to~~ / **apply for** the position of Senior Sales Consultant, as advertised on your website.

I have **worked on** / **worked in** the sales industry for more than eight years, and am **trained in** / **trained of** selling a range of products to varied markets. In my current position, I am **responsible of** / **responsible for** sales to Asian markets, and last year I **looked up** / **looked after** the new market of China, where sales **amounted to** / **amounted on** more than $10 million.

I am **passionate for** / **passionate about** working in the sales industry and welcome the opportunity to learn new skills. I run the training program for new staff members and ten of the junior sales consultants **report to** / **report on** me. In their training, I **focus in** / **focus on** developing awareness of the most effective sales strategies.

Please find my résumé and references attached. I look **forward at** / **forward to** hearing from you.

Yours sincerely,
Deepak Singh

32 Job interviews

In a job interview, it is important to describe your achievements in a specific and detailed way. You can use relative clauses to do this.

🔧 **New language** Relative clauses
Aa Vocabulary Job interviews
🧩 **New skill** Describing your achievements in detail

32.1 CROSS OUT THE INCORRECT WORDS IN EACH SENTENCE

 This is the app ~~who~~ / that / ~~what~~ I designed for the new client.

① The person who / what / which I admire the most in the company is the Sales Manager.

② The office that / which / where I work is a tall, modern building.

③ The customers what / who / why gave us feedback were all very positive.

④ The team that / what / where I lead is fully qualified and highly motivated.

🔊

32.2 MATCH THE BEGINNINGS OF THE SENTENCES TO THE CORRECT ENDINGS

We work with clients	that are designed by IT specialists.
① We sell apps	who have high standards.
② We are based in an office	who want innovative products.
③ I work with clients	where we sell the most.
④ This is the reason	that is in the business park.
⑤ Spain and Italy are the countries	that I applied for this job.

🔊

32.3 REWRITE THE SENTENCES, CORRECTING THE ERRORS

> In my previous job, what was in sales, I learned a lot from my boss.
> *In my previous job, which was in sales, I learned a lot from my boss.*

1 Training staff, that is my favorite part of the job, is really interesting.

_____

2 In my current job, who I serve lots of customers, I have learned how to deal with complaints.

_____

3 My boss, which is very understanding, encourages me to leave the office on time.

_____

4 While I was in college I worked in a café, what taught me a lot about customer service.

_____

 32.4 LISTEN TO THE AUDIO, THEN NUMBER THE PICTURES IN THE ORDER THEY ARE DESCRIBED

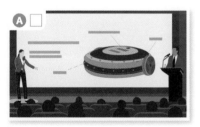

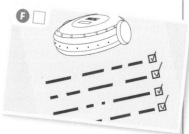

32.5 FILL IN THE GAPS USING THE WORDS IN THE PANEL

The sales team, _whose_ staff work very hard, always meet their targets.

1. Last summer, _____ I had just graduated, I worked as an intern in a bank.

2. My teacher, _____ was an amazing person, inspired me to study law.

3. My apprenticeship, _____ I completed in 2016, was in IT.

4. The place _____ I want to work as a tour guide is New York.

| who | where | ~~whose~~ | which | when |

32.6 MARK THE SENTENCES THAT ARE CORRECT

In 2014, when I had just graduated, I worked as an intern. ☑
In 2014, which I had just graduated, I worked as an intern. ☐

1. Tom's team, who staff are hard-working, hit their sales targets last month. ☐
   Tom's team, whose staff are hard-working, hit their sales targets last month. ☐

2. In my previous job, which was in sales, I learned to give presentations. ☐
   In my previous job, what was in sales, I learned to give presentations. ☐

3. I sometimes work from home as it is the place which I can concentrate best. ☐
   I sometimes work from home as it is the place where I can concentrate best. ☐

4. My clients, who expect good customer service, said my work was excellent. ☐
   My clients, whose expect good customer service, said my work was excellent. ☐

What experience do you have of customer service?

I work with clients _____*who expect*_____ excellent service at all times.

1 What do you like most about your job?

The thing _____ me excited is when we hit our sales targets.

2 What would you say is your biggest strength?

People _____ me well say I am customer-focused and give good customer service.

3 What do you think you would bring to our company?

I have a can-do attitude, _____ that I get things done.

4 What are your salary expectations?

I would hope to receive more than my current salary, _____ $45,000 a year.

5 How soon can you start, supposing we offer you the job?

My boss, _____ quite understanding, would allow me to leave after a month's notice.

| that gets | who know | ~~who expect~~ | which is | who is | which means |

33 Vocabulary

33.1 BUSINESS IDIOMS WRITE THE PHRASES FROM THE PANEL UNDER THE CORRECT DEFINITIONS

To agree totally

to see eye to eye

1 To talk to someone briefly in order to catch up or get an update

3 A strategy worked out beforehand

4 To be in agreement about something

6 Operating properly

7 Simply and succinctly

9 To start doing a job or role that someone else has just left

10 Original and a big departure from what was there before

12 To stop the current activity

13 To do something in a cheaper or easier way, at the expense of high standards

15 A rough estimate

16 To do something strictly according to the rules

2 An increase or decrease in speed from what is normal

_____

5 Uncertain and undecided

_____

8 To make more effort than is usually expected

_____

11 To confirm or settle an agreement or contract

_____

14 To be ahead of your competitors in a certain field

_____

17 To have control of a particular market

_____

a ballpark figure   to touch base

in a nutshell   to go the extra mile

a change of pace   to corner the market

to be ahead of the game   to cut corners

~~to see eye to eye~~   to clinch the deal

to fill someone's shoes   groundbreaking

to do something by the book

a game plan   up in the air

to be on the same page   up and running

to call it a day

34 Working relationships

Phrasal verbs are commonly used to talk about relationships with co-workers and clients. It is important to use the correct word order with phrasal verbs.

⚙ **New language** Three-word phrasal verbs
Aa Vocabulary Social media
🧩 **New skill** Social networking

⚙ 34.1 FILL IN THE GAPS USING THE WORDS IN THE PANEL

My team looks ____*up*____ to me.

1 Alex comes up _____ great ideas.

2 Hal looks down _____ his co-workers.

3 I'm _____ forward to the launch.

4 Fred _____ up with a lot of noise.

5 She comes _____ as rather superior.

6 The printer has run _____ of paper.

7 Jim's staff get _____ with being late.

8 Shona has to _____ up to poor sales.

9 We need to _____ up with the schedule.

across	face	with
puts	~~up~~	on	keep
away	looking	out	

🔊

⚙ 34.2 REWRITE THE SENTENCES, PUTTING THE WORDS IN THE CORRECT ORDER

them. | down | looks | on | John

John looks down on them.

1 my | team. | get | with | I | along

_____

2 friendly. | across | She | as | comes

_____

3 with | I | put | music! | up | can't | his

_____

4 with | good | comes | ideas. | He | up

_____

5 gets | with | lot. | Tom | away | a

_____

6 out | We | run | have | of | coffee.

_____

7 to | We | facts. | must | up | face

_____

🔊

116

34.3 READ THE WEB PAGE AND WRITE ANSWERS TO THE QUESTIONS AS FULL SENTENCES

Business Tips

HOME | ENTRIES | ABOUT | CONTACT

Keeping up with competitors

Some companies have been slow to get up to speed with using social media to strengthen their brand. Some even look down on using social media as trivial and having no value in the business world, but they do so at their own risk. With social media you can reach out to a wider audience and keep up with the latest trends.

Here at ABC Foods we use social media to tell our customers our news. We have previews of our TV ads, so subscribers feel they are keeping up with our news and developments.

We also run competitions that make us stand out from our competitors. Last month, we asked our subscribers to post recipes they had come up with using their favorite ABC foods. We then had customers like their favorite recipes and the best three won prizes.

Using social media in such ways allows us to build loyal customer relationships. Customer loyalty is key to us as loyal customers make repeat purchases. We have to constantly be coming up with new features for our social media activity. Perhaps you have an idea for our next competition!

RECIPE OF THE WEEK

What can social media help you do?

It can help you strengthen your brand.

1 Why don't some companies like social media?

_____

2 Why is it a risk to ignore social media?

_____

3 Why does ABC Foods use social media?

_____

4 What does ABC Foods have previews of?

_____

5 Why does the company do this?

_____

6 Why does ABC Foods run competitions?

_____

7 Why is customer loyalty so important?

_____

34.4 REWRITE THE SENTENCES USING OBJECT PRONOUNS

> You must check out their website.
> *You must check it out.*

1 I'll look up our competitors online.

_____

2 Can you fill in this form?

_____

3 I'd like you to take on this task.

_____

4 I can't let down our clients.

_____

5 Can we talk over your problem?

_____

6 Could you look over my résumé?

_____

7 We are giving away free books.

_____

8 I need to call off our meeting.

_____

9 I can't figure out these sales figures.

_____

10 The taxi will pick up Tom.

_____

11 I keep putting off writing my report.

_____

12 Yola turned down the job offer.

_____

🔊

34.5 LISTEN TO THE AUDIO AND ANSWER THE QUESTIONS

Bilal is giving a presentation on using social media in business.

What should you encourage clients to do?
Look at your website ✓
Take on difficult tasks ☐
Sell your products ☐

1 What do you need to do regularly?
Be in the news ☐
Update your website ☐
Focus on selling ☐

2 What do customers expect from business social media sites?
To find new ideas for your product ☐
To buy more of your products ☐
To read old news stories ☐

3 What is vital for small businesses?
Missing out on opportunities ☐
Translating social media use into sales ☐
Advertising on social media ☐

4 How do successful businesses engage with their target customers?
Uploading photos of their products ☐
Entering competitions ☐
Sharing users' questions and answers ☐

34.6 MATCH THE PICTURES TO THE CORRECT SENTENCES

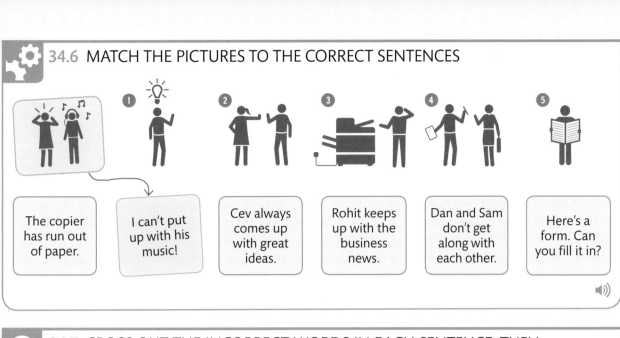

The copier has run out of paper.

I can't put up with his music!

Cev always comes up with great ideas.

Rohit keeps up with the business news.

Dan and Sam don't get along with each other.

Here's a form. Can you fill it in?

34.7 CROSS OUT THE INCORRECT WORDS IN EACH SENTENCE, THEN SAY THE SENTENCES OUT LOUD

They have a new website. Can you ~~check out it~~ / **check it out**?

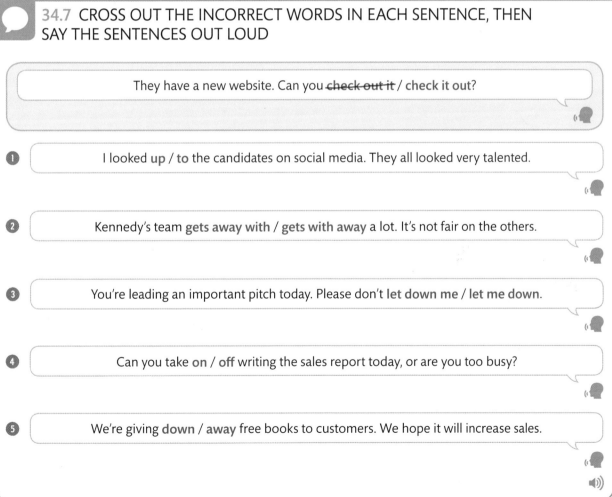

1. I looked **up** / **to** the candidates on social media. They all looked very talented.

2. Kennedy's team **gets away with** / **gets with away** a lot. It's not fair on the others.

3. You're leading an important pitch today. Please don't **let down me** / **let me down**.

4. Can you take **on** / **off** writing the sales report today, or are you too busy?

5. We're giving **down** / **away** free books to customers. We hope it will increase sales.

35 Career outcomes

To talk about possible future events, such as career development and promotion, use "will," "might," and "won't" to say how likely something is to happen.

⚙ **New language** Modal verbs for possibility
Aa Vocabulary Career development
🧩 **New skill** Talking about the future

35.1 MATCH THE PAIRS OF SENTENCES

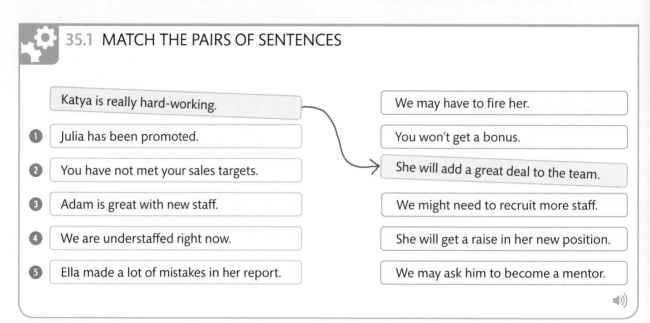

Katya is really hard-working.

1 Julia has been promoted.

2 You have not met your sales targets.

3 Adam is great with new staff.

4 We are understaffed right now.

5 Ella made a lot of mistakes in her report.

We may have to fire her.

You won't get a bonus.

She will add a great deal to the team.

We might need to recruit more staff.

She will get a raise in her new position.

We may ask him to become a mentor.

🔊

35.2 LISTEN TO THE AUDIO AND ANSWER THE QUESTIONS

Ruth is having her annual performance review with her manager, Tim.

Ruth won't meet her sales targets.
True ☐ **False** ☑

1 Ruth will be promoted this year.
True ☐ **False** ☐

2 Ruth may get a company car.
True ☐ **False** ☐

3 Ruth might not be a team leader.
True ☐ **False** ☐

4 Ruth will travel outside the US for work.
True ☐ **False** ☐

5 Ruth might work in the Dallas office.
True ☐ **False** ☐

35.3 MARK THE SENTENCES THAT ARE CORRECT

The company has made a loss this year. You will get a bonus. ☐
The company has made a loss this year. You might not get a bonus. ☑

1 Our staff can't use the new database. We might have to provide more training. ☐
Our staff can't use the new database. We won't have to provide more training. ☐

2 David has over 15 years' experience and he will lead our marketing department. ☐
David has over 15 years' experience and he won't lead our marketing department. ☐

3 I need your report by Thursday. You need might to work overtime. ☐
I need your report by Thursday. You might need to work overtime. ☐

4 Anna's laptop is broken. She wills get a new one this week. ☐
Anna's laptop is broken. She will get a new one this week. ☐

5 There is a pay freeze at the moment, so you won't get a raise. ☐
There is a pay freeze at the moment, so you will get a raise. ☐

6 If Rita's work doesn't get better, we won't have to fire her. ☐
If Rita's work doesn't get better, we may have to fire her. ☐

7 We have some meetings in France. You may have to go to Paris. ☐
We have some meetings in France. You don't may have to go to Paris. ☐

8 We can't hire any staff at the moment, so you don't might get an assistant until March. ☐
We can't hire any staff at the moment, so you might not get an assistant until March. ☐

9 If your presentation goes well, the CEO might ask you to give it to the board. ☐
If your presentation goes well, the CEO won't ask you to give it to the board. ☐

10 Tanya has been promoted. She will lead a team next year. ☐
Tanya has been promoted. She will to lead a team next year. ☐

11 Dev has had a bad trading year. He will meet his sales targets. ☐
Dev has had a bad trading year. He won't meet his sales targets. ☐

12 Paula always goes the extra mile. She will make a great addition to the team. ☐
Paula always goes the extra mile. She won't make a great addition to the team. ☐

◄))

121

35.4 REWRITE THE SENTENCES, PUTTING THE WORDS IN THE CORRECT ORDER

will | bonus | probably. | You | a | get

You will probably get a bonus.

1 promoted. | will | definitely | He | be

_____

2 probably | raise. | You | a | will | get

_____

3 need | She | training. | probably | won't

_____

4 bonus. | They'll | a | get | definitely

_____

5 I | go | won't | vacation. | probably | on

_____

6 I | jobs. | definitely | change | won't

_____

7 We | intern. | hire | an | probably | will

_____

8 He | meet | probably | clients. | won't

_____

9 sell | It | definitely | well. | will

_____

◀))

35.5 SAY THE SENTENCES OUT LOUD, PUTTING THE MODIFIER IN THE CORRECT PLACE

You won't be promoted. [definitely]

You definitely won't be promoted. ◀

1 You will be promoted. [probably]

◀

2 He will get the job. [definitely]

◀

3 She won't get a raise. [definitely]

◀

4 They will get a bonus. [probably]

◀

5 I won't get a new laptop. [probably]

◀

6 You will get a company car. [definitely]

◀

7 I will move to the head office. [probably]

◀

8 You won't need much training. [probably]

◀

9 We will hire a new assistant soon. [definitely]

◀

◀))

35.6 CROSS OUT THE INCORRECT WORDS IN EACH SENTENCE

Everything's up in the air right now. We **might not** / ~~will definitely~~ meet our deadline.

❶ Katrina doesn't have much experience. She **will probably** / **definitely won't** need more training.

❷ Meliz has to travel to see clients. She **definitely won't** / **will probably** get a company car.

❸ Mr. Cox has complained about our service. He **probably won't** / **definitely will** use us again.

❹ The negotiations are going quite well. We **definitely won't** / **might** clinch the deal tomorrow.

❺ You're doing a great job, but our profits are down. You **might not** / **definitely will** get a raise.

🔊

 35.7 READ THE PERFORMANCE REVIEW AND WRITE ANSWERS TO THE QUESTIONS AS FULL SENTENCES

What is Isaac's work like?
Isaac's work is very thorough.

❶ What did Isaac do this year?

_____

❷ What might happen to Isaac next year?

_____

❸ Who will Isaac mentor from next month?

_____

❹ Where will Isaac start selling products?

_____

❺ What might Isaac need in his new role?

_____

❻ How does the company think he will perform?

_____

Name: Isaac Hawkins
Position: Sales adviser
Subject: Performance review

Isaac has worked in our sales department for four years and has a positive attitude. His work is very thorough and he never cuts corners. He met all his sales targets this year, so he will be considered for promotion next year. He is great with new staff and will mentor two new employees from next month. Isaac has shown himself to be a confident and competent sales adviser and from next month will take on sales to Asia after working in the European department for two years. We may need to give Isaac additional training in this field and I am confident he will perform well in this role.

36 Vocabulary

Aa 36.1 OFFICE AND PRESENTATION EQUIPMENT WRITE THE WORDS FROM THE PANEL UNDER THE CORRECT PICTURES

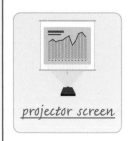

projector screen

① _____

② _____

③ _____

④ _____

⑥ _____

⑦ _____

⑧ _____

⑨ _____

⑩ _____

⑫ _____

⑬ _____

⑭ _____

⑮ _____

⑯ _____

⑱ _____

⑲ _____

⑳ _____

㉑ _____

㉒ _____

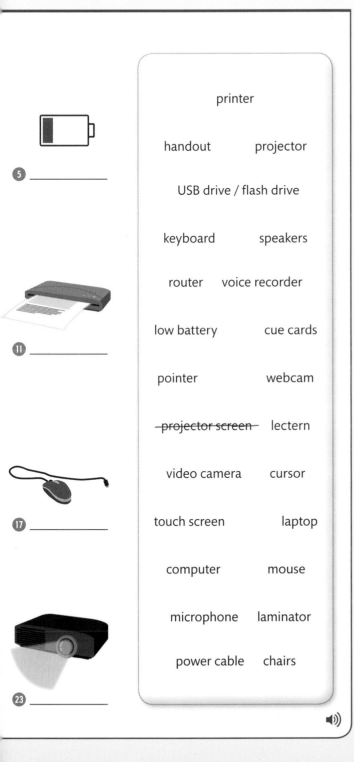

printer

handout   projector

USB drive / flash drive

keyboard   speakers

router   voice recorder

low battery   cue cards

pointer   webcam

~~projector screen~~   lectern

video camera   cursor

touch screen   laptop

computer   mouse

microphone   laminator

power cable   chairs

5 _____

11 _____

17 _____

23 _____

table

flow chart

pie chart

report

~~table~~

graph

1 _____

2 _____

3 _____

4 _____

37 Structuring a presentation

When you are presenting to an audience, it is important to structure your talk in a way that is clear and easy to understand. Certain set phrases can help you do this.

⚙ New language Signposting language
Aa Vocabulary Presentation types
🧩 New skill Structuring a presentation

⚙ 37.1 REWRITE THE SENTENCES, PUTTING THE WORDS IN THE CORRECT ORDER

talk. | to | brings | the | That | end | of | me | my

That brings me to the end of my talk.

① turn | now | prospects. | to | Let's | future

_____

② talk | loyalty. | today | building | is | My | about | brand

_____

③ feel | me. | free | your | Do | tweet | questions | to | to

_____

④ market | we've | at | So, | our | looked | penetration.

_____

⑤ sum | difficult. | up, | been | has | this | To | year

_____

⑥ questions. | and | at | case | We'll | I'll | studies, | look | take | then

_____

⑦ purpose | share | sales | of | is | figures. | talk | to | this | The

_____

🔊

37.2 SAY THE SENTENCES OUT LOUD, FILLING IN THE GAPS USING THE WORDS IN THE PANEL

I'll quickly explain the latest proposal, and ___*then*___ I'll go through some case studies.

1. To _____ up, it's been a very successful year for us.

2. We'll _____ at the competitor's products, then I'll introduce our new product.

3. Do _____ free to interrupt if you'd like to comment.

4. So, we've _____ at problems we need to overcome.

5. Now let's _____ to the solutions to those problems.

| feel | look | ~~then~~ | looked | sum | turn |

Aa 37.3 MATCH THE DEFINITIONS TO THE EQUIPMENT

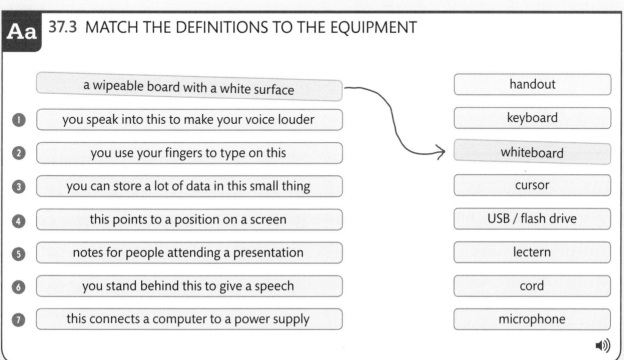

a wipeable board with a white surface → whiteboard

1. you speak into this to make your voice louder — handout
2. you use your fingers to type on this — keyboard
3. you can store a lot of data in this small thing — whiteboard
4. this points to a position on a screen — cursor
5. notes for people attending a presentation — USB / flash drive
6. you stand behind this to give a speech — lectern
7. this connects a computer to a power supply — cord

microphone

37.4 READ THE ARTICLE AND ANSWER THE QUESTIONS

Presentation equipment is always a good idea.
True ☐ **False** ☑ **Not given** ☐

1 Most people do not practice their presentations.
True ☐ **False** ☐ **Not given** ☐

2 It is not important to practice your presentation.
True ☐ **False** ☐ **Not given** ☐

3 It doesn't take long to check your equipment.
True ☐ **False** ☐ **Not given** ☐

4 You should not use built-in cameras too often.
True ☐ **False** ☐ **Not given** ☐

5 The aim of a presentation is to convey a message.
True ☐ **False** ☐ **Not given** ☐

6 It is not always necessary to use lots of equipment.
True ☐ **False** ☐ **Not given** ☐

WELL PRESENTED

Using equipment in presentations can be useful, but it can also make you look unprofessional if you don't know how to use it correctly.

• Practice! Don't leave it until the day to work out how to use the projector screen. Have two or three dry runs to resolve any problems so that your presentation is smooth and professional.

• Make sure equipment is working! Charge any batteries, make sure cords are plugged into sockets and test built-in cameras to make sure they are working, especially if you only use them now and again.

• Don't forget the handouts. High-tech equipment may be great, but the most important thing is that your audience understands the message.

• Sometimes, less is more. If you're not familiar with presentation software, and you fumble when using the remote and pointers, you may be better off not using any visual aids at all. Make your presentation interesting, and whatever you use should be enough.

37.5 LISTEN TO THE AUDIO, THEN NUMBER THE SENTENCES IN THE ORDER YOU HEAR THEM

An HR manager is talking to staff about changes in the company's technology policies.

A They're small, they're light, and they have a built-in camera. ☐

B Many of you need to respond to emails out of the office. ☐

C That's the end of my talk. Do feel free to ask any questions. ☐

D Let's now turn to how this will happen. You will receive an email with a time allocation. ☐

E Good morning, everyone. On your chairs, you should have a handout. ☐ 1

F Now, all of you already have company laptops. Next month you'll also be issued with tablets. ☐

G To sum up, we want to make it as easy and efficient as possible for you to do your jobs. ☐

38 Developing an argument

When you are making a presentation, there are several key phrases you can use to develop your argument, and make your audience aware of what is coming.

New language Useful presentation language
Aa Vocabulary Presentations
New skill Developing an argument

38.1 REWRITE THE SENTENCES, PUTTING THE WORDS IN THE CORRECT ORDER

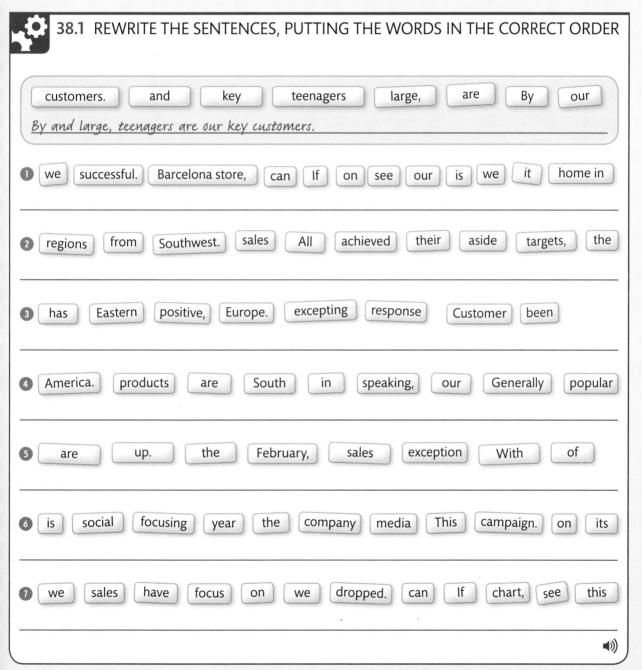

| customers. | and | key | teenagers | large, | are | By | our |

By and large, teenagers are our key customers.

1. we | successful. | Barcelona store, | can | If | on | see | our | is | we | it | home in

_____

2. regions | from | Southwest. | sales | All | achieved | their | aside | targets, | the

_____

3. has | Eastern | positive, | Europe. | excepting | response | Customer | been

_____

4. America. | products | are | South | in | speaking, | our | Generally | popular

_____

5. are | up. | the | February, | sales | exception | With | of

_____

6. is | social | focusing | year | the | company | media | This | campaign. | on | its

_____

7. we | sales | have | focus | on | we | dropped. | can | If | chart, | see | this

_____

38.2 MATCH THE BEGINNINGS OF THE SENTENCES TO THE CORRECT ENDINGS

If we focus on these results → we can see a general trend downward.

to our magazines is falling.

as dealing with customers.

1. Excepting East Asia, our sales

2. In actual fact, the consumer group said

3. As a matter of fact, I don't think

they really liked our prototype.

4. For instance, we've had a lot of positive

many areas where we can improve.

5. In general, the number of subscribers

have grown by more than 10 percent.

6. Concentrating on the basics, there are

feedback about our menswear.

7. Jorge needs to improve key skills such

Alyssa is suitable for the role.

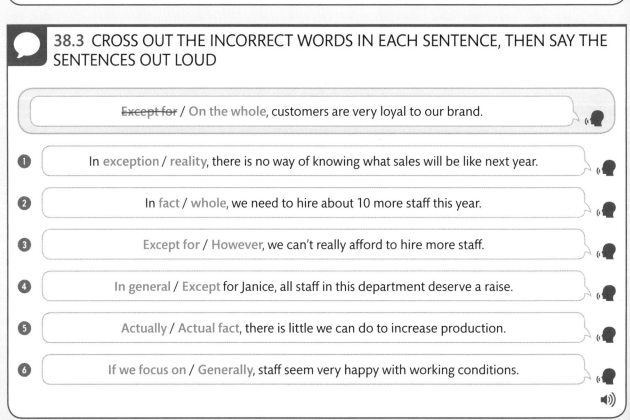

38.3 CROSS OUT THE INCORRECT WORDS IN EACH SENTENCE, THEN SAY THE SENTENCES OUT LOUD

~~Except for~~ / On the whole, customers are very loyal to our brand.

1. In exception / reality, there is no way of knowing what sales will be like next year.

2. In fact / whole, we need to hire about 10 more staff this year.

3. Except for / However, we can't really afford to hire more staff.

4. In general / Except for Janice, all staff in this department deserve a raise.

5. Actually / Actual fact, there is little we can do to increase production.

6. If we focus on / Generally, staff seem very happy with working conditions.

38.4 READ THE ARTICLE AND ANSWER THE QUESTIONS

At the start of a presentation, give a summary.
True ☑ False ☐ Not given ☐

1 It's important to pack your talk full of details.
True ☐ False ☐ Not given ☐

2 It's best to speak in a dramatic way.
True ☐ False ☐ Not given ☐

3 You can end your presentation by giving advice.
True ☐ False ☐ Not given ☐

4 You should invite the audience to ask questions.
True ☐ False ☐ Not given ☐

5 The ideal length for a presentation is 5 minutes.
True ☐ False ☐ Not given ☐

6 Quality is more important than quantity.
True ☐ False ☐ Not given ☐

PRESENTING PROFESSIONALLY

Your boss asks you to give a presentation, but you don't know where to start. Here are our top tips.

✓ On the whole, you should begin your presentation with a summary statement: explain what issue you are addressing and what your presentation will contain.

✓ Home in on key trends. By and large, you don't need to talk about every single detail of an issue. In fact, it's much better to summarize the most important information, or the most dramatic results.

✓ In general, you should end with a recommendation or conclusion. What do you think your company should do in the future? How can they solve a problem or work more efficiently? You can also ask your audience a question: give them something to think about.

✓ Keep it brief. It's much better to give an excellent 5-minute presentation than to give a boring talk for 30 minutes.

 38.5 FILL IN THE GAPS USING THE WORDS IN THE PANEL

In actual _fact_ , Simone has never been late.

1 If we _____ in on profits, we can see growth.

2 If we focus _____ prices, it's clear they're too high.

3 _____ and large, our T-shirts are our bestseller.

4 In _____ , there's no way we can recover.

5 As a _____ of fact, I am very disappointed.

6 Except _____ Korea, I've been to most of Asia.

7 _____ general, China is our biggest market.

| reality | matter | In | home | ~~fact~~ | on | for | By |

39 Pitching a product

When describing a product to a potential client, it is useful to compare the product with competitors using comparative and superlative adjectives.

⚙ **New language** Comparatives and superlatives
Aa Vocabulary Product marketing
🧩 **New skill** Comparing products

⚙ 39.1 CROSS OUT THE INCORRECT WORDS IN EACH SENTENCE

 Our new tablet is **slimmer** / ~~more slim~~ than any other tablet on the market.

① This sports car is **the fastest** / **the most fast** car on sale today.

② Our leather jackets are **fashionable** / **more fashionable** than our competitors' jackets.

③ This digital camera is **the best** / **best** model ever.

④ Our new microwave oven is more efficient **than** / **then** any other model.

⑤ This ice cream maker is **easyer** / **easier** to use than any other on the market.

⑥ Our customers said our sofa is **more comfortable** / **comfortabler** than other models.

⑦ Our organic vegetables are **more fresher** / **fresher** than supermarket vegetables.

⑧ Book a train trip with us in advance to get **the most cheapest** / **the cheapest** fares.

⑨ Our cake range was voted **the tastiest** / **tastiest** on the market in a recent survey.

⑩ These batteries last **more long** / **longer** than the leading brand.

⑪ We think our new winter coat is **the most warm** / **the warmest** on the market.

◀))

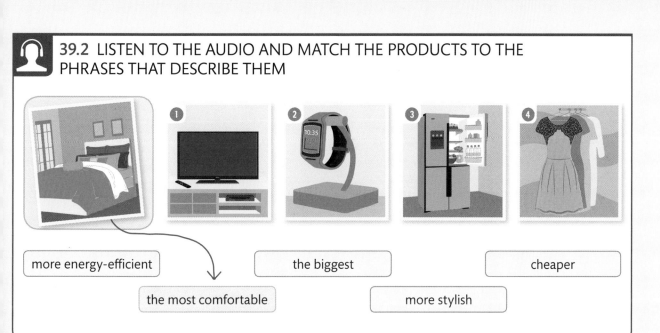

39.2 LISTEN TO THE AUDIO AND MATCH THE PRODUCTS TO THE PHRASES THAT DESCRIBE THEM

more energy-efficient

the most comfortable

the biggest

more stylish

cheaper

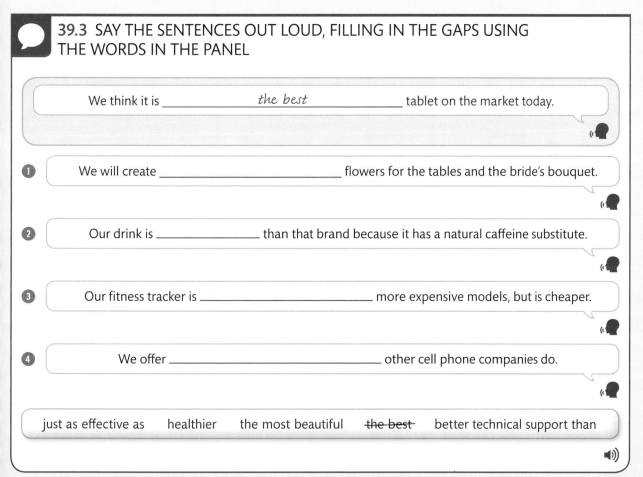

39.3 SAY THE SENTENCES OUT LOUD, FILLING IN THE GAPS USING THE WORDS IN THE PANEL

We think it is _____ *the best* _____ tablet on the market today.

1 We will create _____ flowers for the tables and the bride's bouquet.

2 Our drink is _____ than that brand because it has a natural caffeine substitute.

3 Our fitness tracker is _____ more expensive models, but is cheaper.

4 We offer _____ other cell phone companies do.

just as effective as   healthier   the most beautiful   ~~the best~~   better technical support than

39.4 REWRITE THE SENTENCES, PUTTING THE WORDS IN THE CORRECT ORDER

detergent | as | effective | expensive | just | is | Our | as | brands. | more | laundry

Our laundry detergent is just as effective as more expensive brands.

1 tasty | cheaper. | is | as | much | the | This | leading | pizza | but | brand, | as

_____

2 other | budget | is | as | the | brands | Our | market. | stylish | on | clothing | as

_____

3 are | good | leader. | dishwasher | the | tablets | These | as | market | as | store-brand

_____

4 is | seen. | action | movie | as | Our | anything | you've | as | exciting | latest | ever

_____

5 not | eco-friendly | good | brand. | liquid | This | is | as | the | leading | dishwashing | as

_____

🔊

 39.5 REWRITE THE HIGHLIGHTED PHRASES, CORRECTING THE ERRORS

more exciting

1 _____

2 _____

3 _____

4 _____

5 _____

6 _____

FOOD MONTHLY

SALAD BOX

Receive delicious vegetables, dressings, and a recipe to make excitinger salads each week!

In our boxes, you'll find all you need to make salads as exciting they can be. We also provide you with a recipe card that tells you how to make five different salads. What could be more simpler? Enjoy a convenienter way to dine in at home.

Our salads are among the healthyest on the market. Every box comes with a nutritional information leaflet so you know you are enjoying the most good food. Our recipe boxes are just as cheaper than shopping in your local supermarket. So what are you waiting for? Place your order today.

40 Talking about facts and figures

When you are making a presentation or writing a report, it is important to describe changes and trends with precise language that sounds natural.

⚙️ **New language** Collocations
Aa Vocabulary Business trends
🧩 **New skill** Describing facts and figures

🎧 **40.1 LISTEN TO THE AUDIO, THEN NUMBER THE TRENDS IN THE ORDER THEY ARE DESCRIBED**

A ☐   B 1   C ☐   D ☐   E ☐   F ☐   G ☐   H ☐

⚙️ **40.2 MATCH THE PAIRS OF SENTENCES THAT MEAN THE SAME THING**

There are fewer customer complaints.	We expect a considerable drop in prices.
① Customer complaints are more common.	The share value has rallied slightly.
② Prices peaked, then fell.	Customer complaints have fallen steadily.
③ The price is going up and down a lot.	There was a sharp rise in the share value.
④ Prices are likely to fall significantly.	The price is fluctuating wildly.
⑤ The share value increased dramatically.	There has been an increase in complaints.
⑥ The share value has improved a bit.	There was a dramatic spike last year.

🔊))

40.3 CROSS OUT THE INCORRECT WORD IN EACH SENTENCE

There was a fall **of** / ~~on~~ more than 13 percent.

① Staff numbers went **for** / **from** 120 to 150.

② **Between** / **To** 15 and 18 percent of stock is unsold.

③ We've experienced a boom **of** / **at** 56 percent.

④ Profits have fallen **by** / **at** 11 percent.

⑤ The share price peaked **on** / **at** $22.

⑥ Complaints doubled **in** / **on** the last quarter.

⑦ Our sale was **from** / **between** May and June.

🔊

40.4 READ THE REPORT AND ANSWER THE QUESTIONS

Profits have fallen because of the political situation.
True ☑ **False** ☐ **Not given** ☐

① Mayvis Homes was established 12 years ago.
True ☐ **False** ☐ **Not given** ☐

② Mayvis Homes' share price dropped in the first quarter.
True ☐ **False** ☐ **Not given** ☐

③ People think Mayvis Homes' share price will climb in the next few months.
True ☐ **False** ☐ **Not given** ☐

④ Customers do not like the latest houses built by Mayvis Homes.
True ☐ **False** ☐ **Not given** ☐

⑤ Last year, there was a sharp rise in Rushington Construction's share price.
True ☐ **False** ☐ **Not given** ☐

⑥ Most of Rushington Construction's work comes from the government.
True ☐ **False** ☐ **Not given** ☐

Gloom in construction sector

The construction sector experienced a difficult first quarter, with share prices in the leading construction companies declining considerably. It is believed that worries about recent political events have contributed to a considerable drop in profits in the sector.

Mayvis Homes, which specializes in residential property for the over-60s, saw its share price fall by 12 percent in the first quarter, and there are fears that it could fall further before the end of the year. CEO Stan Gilmore said that customers are adopting a "wait and see" approach before making the decision to buy.

Going against the general trend is Rushington Construction PLC, which focuses on the education and healthcare sectors. Although the company's share price fluctuated slightly last year, the first quarter saw a return to stability, with the company's share price rallying slightly in the first quarter. The company relies on government contracts for between 60 and 85 percent of its work, and therefore is not so affected by short-term market trends.

40.5 RESPOND OUT LOUD TO THE AUDIO, FILLING IN THE GAPS USING THE WORDS IN THE PANEL

What are you doing about customer service staff?

We are increasing our customer service staff from __10 to 15__ .

① What's happening to the price of rice?

There's been a _____ because of a poor harvest.

② When was your best sales period last year?

Our sales _____ $200,000 a day in December.

③ Your production facility seems very efficient.

Yes, malfunctions have _____ since last year.

④ How much of the stock is on sale?

Between _____ percent of our stock is on sale.

⑤ Are you happy with our profits this year?

Yes, they've _____ since last year.

⑥ Why have our costs gone up?

There was an _____ 10 percent in the cost of electricity.

10 to 15	20 and 30	dramatic spike	fallen steadily
increase of	peaked at	rallied slightly	

41 Plans and suggestions

English uses modal verbs to make suggestions, and indirect questions or the passive voice to politely request information or point out a mistake.

⚙ New language Indirect questions
Aa Vocabulary Business negotiations
Ｐ New skill Negotiating politely

Aa 41.1 MATCH THE BEGINNINGS OF THE SENTENCES TO THE CORRECT ENDINGS

Would you mind bringing → the delivery date forward by a week?

1. Are you able to pay — our fee in installments?

2. We might move forward with the contract — as soon as possible.

3. I would like to resolve this issue — that you could design our new logo.

4. Maybe we could discuss some — if you would consider buying in bulk.

5. We were thinking — something more innovative.

6. I'm afraid I was hoping for — alternative options for the design.

🔊

🎧 41.2 LISTEN TO THE AUDIO, THEN NUMBER THE SENTENCES IN THE ORDER YOU HEAR THEM

Pippa is negotiating with a client over her contract to redecorate his store.

Ⓐ Well, we were hoping for something more modern. ☐

Ⓑ I'm afraid we need it sooner. ☐

Ⓒ I was wondering what sort of look you want. ☐ 1

Ⓓ Would you mind waiting until next month for payment? ☐

Ⓔ I was thinking we could use the company colors. ☐

Ⓕ Are you able to pay in installments? ☐

41.3 REWRITE THE INDIRECT QUESTIONS, PUTTING THE WORDS IN THE CORRECT ORDER

tell   Could   expect   me   you   deliver   order?   to   you   our   when

Could you tell me when you expect to deliver our order?

1. try   wondering   I   these   on.   was   where   clothes   I   can

_____

2. me   sample   you   tell   will   when   ready?   designs   be   the   Could

_____

3. I   to   Samia's   I   about   if   you   was   talk   performance.   could   wondering

_____

4. tell   store?   product   you   me   I   order   Could   this   in   whether   can

_____

5. have   whether   invoice   was   my   you   wondering   paid   yet.   I

_____

6. tell   the   Could   is?   me   warranty   you   period   what

_____

7. how   new   from   was   the   I   product   is   one.   wondering   old   different   the

_____

8. when   you   price   available?   will   me   the   Could   be   tell   list

_____

9. able   be   I   offer   if   was   a   wondering   to   me   discount.   would   you

_____

🔊

41.4 REWRITE THE SENTENCES USING THE PASSIVE VOICE

I'm afraid you didn't pay our invoice on time.
I'm afraid our invoice wasn't paid on time.

1 I'm afraid you missed our deadline.
_____

2 It looks as if you sent the wrong size.
_____

3 It seems that you did not apply the discount.
_____

4 I'm afraid you delivered our order to the wrong address.
_____

5 It looks as if you calculated the price incorrectly.
_____

6 It seems that you do not train your employees very well.
_____

7 I'm afraid you did not satisfy our customers.
_____

8 It seems that you lost my order while it was being delivered.
_____

9 I'm afraid you did not cook my steak properly.
_____

10 It looks as if you have made a mistake.
_____

11 It seems that you still haven't fixed the printer.
_____

12 I'm afraid you did not check the document thoroughly enough.
_____

◀))

41.5 CROSS OUT THE INCORRECT WORDS IN EACH SENTENCE, THEN SAY THE SENTENCES OUT LOUD

Could / ~~Do~~ you tell me when my order will be ready?

1. I was wondering if **you could** / **could you** look at my presentation.

2. Could you **tell** / **telling** me when my order will be dispatched?

3. I was wondering if you **do** / **would** be free to meet tomorrow.

4. Could you tell me when **can we** / **we can** expect our invoice to be paid?

5. I was wondering what time **does the store open** / **the store opens**.

6. Could you **tell me** / **know** how much the new product should retail for?

41.6 READ THE EMAIL AND MARK THE CORRECT SUMMARY

1. Juanita has only paid 25 percent of Brendan's invoice because she is not happy with the service she received. She wants the staff to receive training. ☐

2. Juanita has not paid Brendan's invoice because she is unhappy with the service that she received. She does not think Brendan has trained his staff well. ☐

3. Brendan has not invoiced Juanita for the bikes because his staff were rude to Juanita. He is going to give them training in customer service. ☐

4. Brendan has sent a revised invoice for the bikes because the order was delivered two weeks late. He is going to look into training his staff. ☐

To: Brendan Schultz

Subject: Late delivery

Dear Mr. Schultz,

I am writing to complain about the poor service we received from your company. We placed an order for 25 bikes, which were due to be delivered on December 2. However, nothing was delivered from you on that date. Your staff did not appear to know anything about our order, which makes me think they must not have been trained properly. The order was delivered two weeks later, which led to us losing sales. We are therefore withholding payment until the situation can be resolved.

Kind regards,

Juanita Estevez

42 Emphasizing your opinion

There are many English phrases for politely emphasizing your point of view. These are useful when you are dealing with disagreement in the workplace.

⚙ **New language** Discourse markers for emphasis
Aa Vocabulary Workplace disagreement
🧩 **New skill** Emphasizing your opinion

⚙ 42.1 MARK THE SENTENCES THAT ARE CORRECT

What we need is an up-to-date delivery schedule from you. ☑
What need is an up-to-date delivery schedule from you. ☐

① If I ask you, you won't find a better deal ☐
If you ask me, you won't find a better deal. ☐

② Actually, we are waiting for the factory to send us more of that product. ☐
We are waiting actually for the factory to send us more of that product. ☐

③ The most thing is that we agree on schedule dates. ☐
The main thing is that we agree on schedule dates. ☐

④ What I'm saying is that I can offer free delivery on orders over a hundred. ☐
What I say is that I can offer free delivery on orders over a hundred. ☐

🔊

🎧 42.2 LISTEN TO THE AUDIO AND ANSWER THE QUESTIONS

Tia is negotiating with a store manager, Roger, who she hopes will sell her new product.

Roger is happy with Tia's asking price.
True ☐ **False** ☑ **Not given** ☐

① The raincoats sell for $30 in the store.
True ☐ **False** ☐ **Not given** ☐

② Roger is happy with Tia's revised deal.
True ☐ **False** ☐ **Not given** ☐

③ Roger places an order for 200 raincoats.
True ☐ **False** ☐ **Not given** ☐

④ The raincoats are the cheapest on the market.
True ☐ **False** ☐ **Not given** ☐

⑤ Tia would sell the raincoats in another store.
True ☐ **False** ☐ **Not given** ☐

Unfortunately, I can't do the job until next month.

That's OK. _The main thing is_ that we have the right person to do the job.

1 Could you send some sample designs for us to look at?

_____ , we sent you an email with them this morning.

2 Is there any way you could offer a reduced asking price?

I'm afraid not. If _____ , this is a great deal.

3 We'd like to sign the contract today if that is possible.

What _____ an assurance that you can meet our schedule dates.

4 Would you consider offering us a discount?

The _____ that we agree on a price that allows enough profit.

5 Can we say a price of $50 per unit?

_____ your asking price is too high. Can we say $40 a unit?

I'm afraid	Actually	~~The main thing is~~
you ask me	main thing is	we need is

143

43 Discussing conditions

English often uses the first and second conditionals for negotiating with clients and co-workers, and the zero conditional to talk about general truths.

⚙️ **New language** Conditionals
Aa Vocabulary Negotiating and bargaining
🧩 **New skill** Discussing possibilities

⚙️ **43.1 FILL IN THE GAPS BY PUTTING THE VERBS IN THE CORRECT FORMS TO MAKE SECOND CONDITIONAL SENTENCES**

> If the contract ____*was*____ (be) clearer, we ___*would sign*___ (sign) it now.

1. If they _____ (give) us a discount, we _____ (place) an order.

2. If the product _____ (be) cheaper, we _____ (buy) it.

3. If they _____ (move) the deadline, we _____ (meet) it.

4. I _____ (reply) to the email now if I _____ (have) more time.

5. We _____ (sell) more online if our website _____ (be) faster.

6. We _____ (send) the package tomorrow if you _____ (order) before 9 tonight.

7. If the agency _____ (send) us better temps, we _____ (use) them again.

8. If I _____ (work) late every night, I _____ (finish) my report for Friday.

9. I _____ (apply) for the job if the hours _____ (not be) so long.

🔊

144

43.2 LISTEN TO THE AUDIO AND ANSWER THE QUESTIONS

Andrés is negotiating with a painting and decorating company about his home improvements.

The team can start in December.
True ☐ **False** ☑ **Not given** ☐

① The team might finish by the end of January.
True ☐ **False** ☐ **Not given** ☐

② There are six painters on the team.
True ☐ **False** ☐ **Not given** ☐

③ Andrés asks the team to repaint all the rooms.
True ☐ **False** ☐ **Not given** ☐

④ Andrés knows what colors he wants.
True ☐ **False** ☐ **Not given** ☐

⑤ Andrés wants to see more wallpaper samples.
True ☐ **False** ☐ **Not given** ☐

⑥ Andrés won't see new designs until next week.
True ☐ **False** ☐ **Not given** ☐

43.3 REWRITE THE ZERO CONDITIONAL SENTENCES, PUTTING THE WORDS IN THE CORRECT ORDER

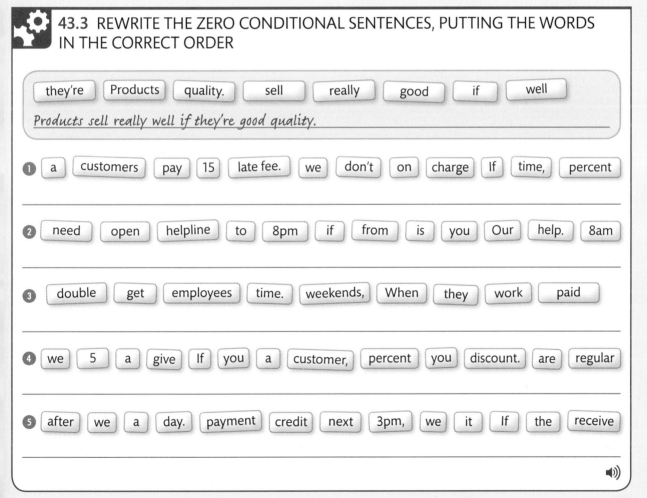

| they're | Products | quality. | sell | really | good | if | well |

Products sell really well if they're good quality.

① | a | customers | pay | 15 | late fee. | we | don't | on | charge | If | time, | percent |

_____

② | need | open | helpline | to | 8pm | if | from | is | you | Our | help. | 8am |

_____

③ | double | get | employees | time. | weekends, | When | they | work | paid |

_____

④ | we | 5 | a | give | If | you | a | customer, | percent | you | discount. | are | regular |

_____

⑤ | after | we | a | day. | payment | credit | next | 3pm, | we | it | If | the | receive |

_____

145

43.4 MATCH THE BEGINNINGS OF THE SENTENCES TO THE CORRECT ENDINGS

If you book 100 places, → we'll give you a 5 percent discount.

1. If you need help with your computer,
2. We would move production to Europe,
3. We will issue a full refund
4. If clients are regular customers,
5. If our receptionist was rude to you,

we would give her a verbal warning.

if it was cheaper to do that.

we'll give you a 5 percent discount.

we give them a 5 percent discount.

you can call the IT department.

if you return the product to one of our stores.

43.5 REWRITE THE FIRST CONDITIONAL SENTENCES, CORRECTING THE ERRORS

If you **will order** before 9pm, we'll deliver your goods the following day.
If you order before 9pm, we'll deliver your goods the following day.

1. If you **not** pay on time, we won't send you your order.

_____

2. We'll issue a full refund if **you won't be** happy with our products.

_____

3. If you **will book** two nights in our hotel, we'll give you a third night for free.

_____

4. If Alan's presentation **will go** well, he will get promoted next month.

_____

5. We won't charge you for your stay if you **won't** get a good night's sleep.

_____

6. If you **ordering** over 100 units, we'll give you a discount.

_____

43.6 RESPOND OUT LOUD TO THE AUDIO, FILLING IN THE GAPS USING THE PHRASES IN THE PANEL

Our standard price for this new model is $200 per unit.

Well, if you lowered the price, ___*I would buy*___ 50 units.

1 We'd like the renovations to be finished by the end of next month.

Well, if you pay for the overtime, _____ the job by then.

2 Is there any possibility you can give us a discount?

Yes. If _____ 100 units or more, we give them a 5 percent discount.

3 I'm not happy with the quality of your product.

If you return it to us within 28 days, _____ a full refund.

4 Our new tablet retails for $79 in all major stores. We can do you a price of $69 per unit.

If _____ a price of $59 per unit, we'd sell it in our stores.

5 Your product is not very good quality.

We're sorry to hear that. If a customer makes a complaint, _____ it very seriously.

6 We love your product. We'd like to place an order for 100 units a month.

We can't do that yet. If _____ on extra staff, we'd be able to increase production.

we take	we will issue	~~I would buy~~	clients buy
we took	we will finish	you could do	

44 Discussing problems

English uses the third conditional to talk about an unreal past, or events that did not happen. This is useful for talking about workplace mistakes.

⚙ **New language** Third conditional
Aa Vocabulary Workplace mistakes
🧩 **New skill** Talking about past mistakes

 44.1 FILL IN THE GAPS BY PUTTING THE VERBS IN THE CORRECT FORMS TO MAKE THIRD CONDITIONAL SENTENCES

If you __had worked__ (work) late, you __would have finished__ (finish) the presentation.

① We _____ (sign) the contract if the deadline _____ (not be) so tight.

② If we _____ (leave) earlier, we _____ (not miss) the train.

③ If the waitress _____ (not be) so rude, we _____ (not complain).

④ If we _____ (order) before 3pm, we _____ (receive) the goods today.

⑤ We _____ (not lose) the client if we _____ (deliver) the report on time.

⑥ If you _____ (repair) the printer, we _____ (not cancel) the contract.

⑦ If I _____ (know) how expensive it was, I _____ (put) it in the safe.

⑧ The boss _____ (not shout) if you _____ (admit) your mistake.

⑨ If you _____ (be) more prepared, you _____ (give) a better presentation.

⑩ We _____ (give) you free delivery if you _____ (pay) on time.

⑪ If I _____ (know) our competitor's price, I _____ (offer) a bigger discount.

⑫ We _____ (meet) our deadline if we _____ (employ) more staff.

⑬ If you _____ (not be) off sick, we _____ (invite) you to the meeting.

⑭ We _____ (pay) the full amount due if you _____ (not miss) our deadline.

⑮ If you _____ (sell) more products last time, we _____ (ask) you to lead the pitch.

🔊

44.2 LISTEN TO THE AUDIO AND MARK WHICH THINGS ACTUALLY HAPPENED

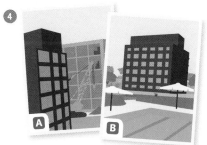

44.3 MATCH THE BEGINNINGS OF THE SENTENCES TO THE CORRECT ENDINGS

If you'd left earlier	we wouldn't have canceled their order.
1 If I'd used the spell check,	he wouldn't have been so angry.
2 If she'd told the boss about her mistake,	you wouldn't have missed the meeting.
3 If they'd paid on time,	my report would have been up to date.
4 If I'd used the latest sales data,	he would have asked for one.
5 If he'd checked the order was right,	we would have given you a discount.
6 If you'd ordered more units,	my work wouldn't have had so many errors.
7 If he'd wanted an older model,	his clients wouldn't have complained.

🔊

44.4 REWRITE THE SENTENCES USING "UNLESS"

> If you don't order 500 units, we won't be able to give you a discount.
> *Unless you order 500 units, we won't be able to give you a discount.*

1 Clive will get a verbal warning if his timekeeping doesn't improve.

_____

2 If you don't pay by the end of today, we will cancel the contract.

_____

3 We won't win the contract if we can't offer a better price.

_____

4 I won't get promoted this year if I don't impress the boss.

_____

5 Your warranty will not be valid if you don't register your product.

_____

6 If I don't sell to 100 new customers, I won't meet my sales targets.

_____

7 We won't make many sales if we don't beat our competitors' prices.

_____

8 If I don't work overtime, I'm not going to meet the deadline.

_____

9 His presentation will be boring if he doesn't add special effects.

_____

10 The CEO won't be happy if we don't win the contract.

_____

11 If you don't lower the price, we won't order any more units.

_____

12 We will miss the train if we don't leave now.

_____

44.5 READ THE REPORT AND ANSWER THE QUESTIONS

The clients were happy with the product.
True ☐ False ☑ Not given ☐

1 Customers wanted recipes from around the world.
True ☐ False ☐ Not given ☐

2 Future Foods didn't offer traditional dishes.
True ☐ False ☐ Not given ☐

3 Customers wanted evening deliveries.
True ☐ False ☐ Not given ☐

4 Customers thought that the price was too high.
True ☐ False ☐ Not given ☐

5 Future Foods will develop more international dishes.
True ☐ False ☐ Not given ☐

PROGRESS REPORT

Ten months ago we launched our new recipe service, Future Foods, where we send customers the ingredients to cook a new recipe. Sales have been very disappointing, and feedback on the service was not as good as we expected.

WHY? Customers said that they prefer to try a range of dishes from around the world. If we had known that, we would have had less of a focus on traditional meals. They also said that the price could be lower.

WHAT NOW? Unless we reduce the price of our service and listen to customers' feedback, we won't make as many sales as we want. We need to offer a more international, affordable range of foods and recipe packs.

44.6 CROSS OUT THE INCORRECT WORDS IN EACH SENTENCE, THEN SAY THE SENTENCES OUT LOUD

If you ~~would have finished~~ / **had finished** the project on time, we wouldn't have lost the client.

1 We would have hit our sales target if the internet **hadn't gone** / **wouldn't have gone** down.

2 If he **had left** / **would leave** earlier, he wouldn't have been late for the meeting.

3 If you had been less rude, we **would have won** / **had won** the contract.

4 The CEO would have promoted me if she **had seen** / **would have seen** my presentation.

5 If we **had lowered** / **would have lowered** the price, we would have made more sales.

Answers

1.1 🔊

❶ I'd like to **introduce** you to Marco from IT.

❷ You **must** be Paola from Madrid.

❸ Gloria, **meet** Julia, our new secretary.

❹ Have you two **met** each other before?

❺ Great to **see** you again!

❻ **Nice** to meet you, Antonio.

❼ Sanjay has **told** me all about you.

❽ I don't **think** we've met before, have we?

❾ It's a **pleasure** to meet you.

1.2 🔊

❶ Simone, I'd like to introduce you to **Gerald, our new sales manager.**

❷ Hello. I don't think we've **met. My name's Jana.**

❸ You must be Selma from the **Chicago branch. Great to meet you.**

❹ Hi, Omar. I think we **met at the conference in Dubai last year.**

❺ My boss has told me **so much about your work.**

❻ This is Colin from IT. **Colin, meet Liam. He's joining our team soon.**

1.3

❶ False

❷ True

❸ Not given

❹ True

❺ False

❻ False

1.4 🔊

❶ I **catch** the train to work at 8:15am each morning.

❷ We **have** a new printer that is difficult to use.

❸ I **am** working at the Guangdong branch all this August.

❹ Sanchez **knows** Katie because they worked together.

❺ **Are** you enjoying this presentation? I think it's great.

❻ Tim **doesn't know** Anna from the Montevideo branch.

❼ Marek **likes** the new furniture we bought for the office.

❽ How **do you spell** your name?

❾ The meeting usually **takes** only half an hour.

❿ Doug is really **enjoying** the conference this year.

⓫ I'd like **to** introduce you to my manager, José Rodriguez.

⓬ Clara **works** from 8:30 to 4:30 on Thursdays and Fridays.

1.5 🔊

❶ Our company **is having** some difficulties at the moment.

❷ Pablo, I'd like you to **meet** my wife, Elvira.

❸ I usually hate conferences, but I **am enjoying** this one a lot.

❹ I **have** two children, a son and a daughter.

❺ Michael, **I'd like** to introduce you to Michelle.

❻ I **don't think** we've met before, have we?

❼ It's so great **to see** you again after such a long time.

❽ How **do you pronounce** your last name?

❾ You must **be** Harold from Copenhagen. Nice to meet you.

❿ Hi, I think we met in Oslo, **didn't we**?

2.1 🔊

❶ I was preparing for the presentation.

❷ Did Greg work in the New York branch?

❸ Akira was living in Kyoto in 1998.

❹ I didn't understand the presentation.

❺ Pete was reading a book at 9pm yesterday.

❻ I was feeling exhausted at work, so I left.

❼ Did you enjoy the presentation?

❽ Were you working in IT then?

❾ Kai wasn't feeling well, so he went home.

❿ I found a new job in France.

2.2

Ⓐ 6

Ⓑ 1

Ⓒ 5

Ⓓ 7

Ⓔ 4

Ⓕ 3

Ⓖ 2

Ⓗ 8

2.3 🔊

❶ Daniel **has worked** for more than five different law firms.

❷ I **have taken** the bus to work all my working life.

❸ The company **has employed** five new people since September.

❹ Peter is a terrible waiter. He **has started** looking for a different job.

❺ Andrea **has worked** here since she graduated in 1999.

❻ The factory **has produced** 15,000 machines this year.

❼ Tim's really happy. He **has finished** his presentation for tomorrow.

8 We **have sold** our products in more than 25 countries.

9 I **have walked** to work since my car broke down.

10 I **have decided** that I'm going to retire next year.

11 Dave **has taken** more time than we expected.

12 I **have worked** at this office for more than 25 years now.

13 Chris **has visited** more than 50 countries so far.

2.4

1 Jim was preparing a presentation **when his boss entered the room**.

2 I've worked at this company **for more than ten years**.

3 Chris had to wait for a taxi for **more than an hour**.

4 Tim moved to New York **when he was transferred to the US office**.

5 I ran my own software company **before I started working here**.

6 In 2013, our company **bought a smaller Canadian software firm**.

2.5

1 True

2 True

3 False

4 True

5 Not given

6 True

2.6 🔊

1 At 3pm yesterday, I **was discussing** the new software with our IT team.

2 While Susan **was eating** lunch, her team was working hard.

3 Karl moved to Berlin when he **lost** his job in Paris.

4 Alan **was traveling** to work when he received a call from his wife.

5 In 2007, I **was working** in the company headquarters in Geneva.

6 I **have lived** in San Francisco since 2003.

7 Peter **was sleeping** at his desk when his phone rang.

8 They **have been** based in Frankfurt since 1994.

9 While I **was living** in France, I worked as a waiter.

10 Derek **bought** his first house in 2009.

11 What **were you doing** at 4pm this afternoon?

12 I **was studying** in college when I decided to work as a lawyer.

13 Who was in the meeting room when you **entered**?

14 We **sold** our first machine in China in 2003.

03

3.1 🔊

1 Human Resources (HR)

2 Information Technology (IT)

3 Sales

4 Public Relations (PR)

5 Legal

6 Facilities / Office Services

7 Administration

8 Research and Development (R&D)

9 Accounts / Finance

10 Marketing

11 Production

3.2 🔊

1 assistant

2 Chief Executive Officer (CEO)

3 Chief Financial Officer (CFO)

4 employee

5 manager

3.3 🔊

1 to work for

2 to work as

3 to be responsible for

4 to be in charge of

5 to work in

04

4.1 🔊

1 Claude is used to working weekends.

2 Did Paul use to work in San Francisco?

3 I am not used to working in such heat.

4 The team used to go out for lunch.

5 We didn't use to have so many meetings.

6 I used to live in a house near the office.

7 Did you use to work in Paris?

8 I'm used to the new software now.

9 I'll never get used to this operating system.

10 Kerry is used to commuting a long way.

4.2

A 7

B 1

C 5

D 6

E 2

F 4

G 3

4.3 🔊

❶ We didn't use to have so much free time.

❷ I'll never get used to driving on the left.

❸ Did Anthony use to work in the Frankfurt branch?

❹ I am used to having to get up at 6am.

❺ Derek isn't used to commuting so far to work.

❻ The team hasn't got used to the new operating system.

❼ We used to have lunch in the café near the park.

❽ Danielle isn't used to giving presentations.

❾ Pam used to work in the branch in Cologne.

❿ Phil isn't used to wearing a uniform for work.

4.4 🔊

❶ She's not used to working long hours.

❷ I used to work as a doctor.

❸ Dan's used to driving on the left.

❹ She's used to getting up early.

❺ I'm not used to spicy food.

❻ I'll never get used to English weather.

❼ I'm not used to working so late.

❽ We're getting used to the new boss.

4.5 🔊

❶ No, thanks. I'm fine.

❷ I'm not used to this hot weather!

❸ That would be great!

❹ I haven't yet. Is it any good?

❺ I'm getting used to the traffic.

4.6 🔊

❶ Are you **used to** living in a tropical country yet?

❷ I **used to** travel to work on foot before they built the metro.

---

❸ When I lived in Berlin, we **used to** live in an apartment downtown.

❹ **Did you use to** work in the Edinburgh branch?

❺ I grew up in Japan, so I'm **used to** driving on the left.

❻ Arnold's **used to** waking up at 5am every morning.

❼ I **am used to** working for a demanding boss.

❽ When I was a child, I didn't **use to** like going to school.

❾ We **used to** go to Florida each year on vacation.

❿ My father **used to** work in a factory until it closed down.

05

5.1 🔊

❶ Staff must not smoke in the building.

❷ We don't have to go to work tomorrow.

❸ I have to go home early on Thursday.

❹ You have to do this assignment today.

❺ We need to increase sales this year.

❻ Jim doesn't have to attend the meeting.

❼ The team must not forget their timesheets.

❽ Paolo has got to sign up for the course.

❾ We will need to hire new staff this fall.

❿ We must improve our productivity.

5.2

❶ False

❷ True

❸ False

❹ False

❺ False

---

❻ Not given

❼ True

❽ True

❾ Not given

5.3 🔊

❶ Would you give Peter a copy of the minutes, please?

❷ All visitors must leave their passes at reception.

❸ Could you take this letter to the post office, please?

❹ Ramon needs to work harder if he wants a promotion.

❺ Sharon needs to sign up for the training course.

❻ Could you leave a copy of the agenda on my desk, please?

❼ You must complete the enrolment form before 5pm on Friday.

❽ Staff must not smoke inside the building.

❾ Would you send an email to everyone about the meeting?

❿ You must finish the project by Wednesday evening.

5.4 🔊

❶ The company must change **if it wants to survive**.

❷ I need you to finish **the presentation by Friday**.

❸ Could you keep a **record of everything you spend this week**?

❹ Would you inform **the team about the recent changes, please**?

❺ The company has got to **invest more in training**.

❻ You don't have **to finish the assignment today**.

❼ We need to think **about closing some of our branches**.

5.5

1. True
2. False
3. Not given
4. False
5. False

5.6 🔊

1. No, I **don't need** you to finish it today.
2. I'm sorry, Mike. We really **must** have it by Friday.
3. I'm sorry, but members of the public **must not** enter the building.
4. We need them tomorrow. **Could** you call the supplier, please?
5. No, you **don't have** to. The deadline is next week.
6. Well, I **need** it by 1pm today.

06

6.1 🔊

1. to make a loss
2. to undercut competitors
3. an overdraft
4. overheads
5. sales figures
6. to get into debt
7. to break even
8. an economic downturn
9. income
10. expenditure / outlay
11. an upturn in the market
12. accounts
13. to drop
14. cash flow
15. to peak
16. the exchange rate
17. to go out of business

07

7.1 🔊

1. Sales **were** good because we **had organized** a good marketing campaign.
2. Sales **had fallen** sharply, so we **decided** to withdraw the product.
3. Aditya **wanted** to try a program that the team **hadn't used / had not used** before.
4. After Peter **had finished** the report, he **wanted** to go on vacation.

7.2 🔊

1. Ramon **had written** ten pages of the report when his computer **crashed**.
2. Many of our employees **had not** visited the factory before and **were** very impressed.
3. Bob's speech **was** disappointing because he **hadn't prepared** well.
4. Nobody **had told** the conference delegates where their hotel **was**.
5. I **hadn't delegated** tasks to Kai before, but I **thought** he did a good job.

7.3 🔊

1. The **following** report will explore our new sales strategy.
2. As can be **seen** in the table, we have invested $4 million this year.
3. Some of our customers have **stated** that they are not satisfied with the result.
4. Our initial investigation **suggests** that this is not true.
5. Our **initial** recommendation is to reduce the budget by 50 percent.
6. We **consulted** a number of focus groups for this report.

7.4 🔊

1. The purpose of our report **is to review our current sales strategy**.
2. The following report presents **a summary of our findings**.
3. Our clients stated that **they were unhappy with the changes**.
4. Based on the initial research, **we should invest more in R&D**.
5. Our principal recommendation is to **proceed with the sale of the subsidiary**.

7.5

1. 20 miles from downtown
2. Rail connections to other cities
3. It is affordable in Alchester
4. Stay in Alchester for over ten years
5. A decision has not yet been made

7.6 🔊

1. The purpose of this report is to compare the two factories.
2. Focus groups had been consulted before we implemented the policy.
3. Sales of our products had fallen in comparison with the previous quarter.
4. Our principal recommendation is to increase investment in R&D.
5. Profits had risen by more than 20 percent in the first half of 2015.

7.7 🔊

1. In this report we will **present** the findings of our research.
2. The **purpose** of this report is to investigate the pros and cons of the new software.
3. This bar chart **compares** the sales figures for the last two years.
4. Our customers **stated** that they had been disappointed with the product.

8.1 🔊
1 Of course. Let me see what I can do.
2 Certainly. It's ZX42 9JL.
3 We've been having difficulties with our software.
4 We'll offer you a discount on your next order.

8.2 🔊
1 Could you **tell me** your reference number?
2 **Let's see** what we can do.
3 **We'll offer** you a full refund.
4 Our driver **has been experiencing** problems.
5 Could you **hold the line**, please?
6 I'm very **sorry to hear** that.
7 Can you **look into** this issue?
8 **We'll send you** a replacement.
9 Of course I can **help** you.

8.3 🔊
1 I'm very **sorry** to hear that, sir.
2 Certainly. Let's **see** what I can do.
3 Could you tell me your **reference** number, please?
4 Could you please **hold** the line?
5 I'm sorry. Our IT system's been **experiencing** difficulties.
6 My order **arrived** dirty and broken.
7 Can you **offer** any compensation?
8 Of course. We'll give you a **discount** on your next order.

8.4 🔊
1 Could you look **into** the problem for me?
2 The company **has** been experiencing difficulties recently.
3 Please **hold** the line for a moment.
4 I've been **waiting** all day for my order to arrive.

8.5 🔊
Note: Answers to 1, 2, and 4 can also be written in contracted form.
1 We **have been preparing** a proposal all evening.
2 Our website **has been experiencing** difficulties this morning.
3 Chris **has been working** on that project for three months now.
4 Our products **have not been selling** well so far this year.

8.6 🔊
1 Peter has been talking for more than 25 minutes.
2 Have you been getting good feedback from the clients?
3 The company has been losing money for years.
4 Juan hasn't been working at our company for long.

8.7
A 4
B 2
C 6
D 5
E 1
F 3

8.8
4

9.1 🔊
1 social media
2 a website
3 automated
4 to access
5 to work online
6 up to date
7 user-friendly
8 to back up
9 a conference call
10 breaking up
11 to download an app
12 a mobile device
13 to work offline
14 an email has bounced
15 to charge
16 a username and password
17 a network

10.1 🔊
1 I hope all's well **with you and the team in Tokyo**.
2 Would you be free **on Thursday July 7 at 4pm**?
3 Please give me a call **if you can't make it**.
4 Please see the schedule **for next week's conference attached**.
5 If you have any questions, **don't hesitate to get in touch**.

10.2 🔊
1 I was **wondering** if you could help me prepare my presentation.
2 Would you be free to **meet** on Thursday evening?

3 I'm **copying** Sanjay and Anita in on this email.
4 I **hope** all's well with you and the team in Delhi.
5 Please see the minutes of yesterday's meeting **attached**.
6 If you have any **questions**, please let me know.
7 How **about** joining us at the pizza place later this evening?

10.3 🔊
1 I just wanted **to** check that you're coming to the presentation.
2 Would you **be** free next Wednesday morning at 11:30?
3 Please find a copy of the report **attached**.
4 If you **have** any questions, please let me know.
5 I'm **copying** Ricardo in on this.

10.4
4

11

11.1 🔊
1 Mohammed **is meeting** the new supplier to discuss a new deal.
2 Jola **is talking** to Sales this afternoon to agree new discounts.
3 They **are aiming** to have the presentation ready by 5:00pm.
4 I **am writing** to inform you that there is a delay with the part you need.
5 We **are still waiting** to hear from the Chinese partners.

11.2
1 Future
2 Future
3 Future
4 Present

11.3
1 hesitate
2 obtain
3 confirm
4 inform
5 prefer
6 assure

11.4 🔊
1 Will you be attending the launch of the new products?
2 I was wondering if we could put our meeting back to tomorrow.
3 We are aiming to send the new designs by Friday.
4 Will you be paying for the order in cash or by card?
5 I was wondering if you would take the clients out for dinner.

11.5 🔊
1 We are still putting together the final sales report.
2 Will you be giving the presentation at tomorrow's conference?
3 We were wondering if we could postpone our meeting.

11.6
1 Not given
2 True
3 False
4 False

12

12.1 🔊
1 Can you deal **with** the cleaners, please? The kitchen is a mess.
2 Can we catch **up** later this morning at around 11:00?
3 Is the fridge broken again? I'll **look** into that now.
4 Have we run **out** of paper? There's none in the photocopier.

12.2 🔊
1 Can we **fix up** a meeting with Marketing and Sales?
2 Have you asked Surina to **fill out** all the paperwork?
3 The printer has **run out** of ink again.
4 I can't **figure out** what Dave wants me to do.
5 I need to **bring up** the topic of punctuality with you.

12.3 🔊
1 I need to **back** my files **up**.
2 Can you **give** the agenda **out**?
3 Can we **call** tomorrow's meeting **off**?
4 Can you **pass** my message **on** to her?
5 Let me **hand** the minutes **out**.
6 I want to **put** my tie **on**.
7 Can you **fix** another meeting **up**?
8 I need to **send** an email **out**.
9 We are **taking** new staff **on**.
10 Can you **set** the projector **up**?
11 I'd like to **talk** the sales plan **over**.

12.4

1 She hasn't backed them up
2 Thursday afternoon
3 Write a report about feedback
4 Deal with some of Amanda's emails
5 A message
6 His best suit and tie

12.5 🔊

1 Jamil's flight is delayed. I think we'll have to call our meeting with him **off**.
2 All employees have to put an apron **on** before entering the kitchen.
3 We're hoping to give **out** samples of our work at the exhibition.
4 It's really important to back your files **up** every night or you could lose work.

12.6 🔊

1 Khalil has **filled the form** out.
2 She has just **hung up** on me without saying goodbye!
3 He **put his tie on** because he had an important meeting.
4 He gave **his report out** to everyone at the meeting.
5 They **set a meeting** up for later in the week.

13

13.1 🔊

1 packaging
2 product testing
3 handmade
4 a one-off production
5 labor-intensive
6 stock
7 product approval
8 raw materials
9 a prototype
10 a production line

11 a warehouse
12 shipping
13 ethically sourced
14 overproduction
15 a factory
16 mass production
17 a supplier

14

14.1 🔊

1 The media **had been** told about the press launch and were out in force.
2 New models **are being** created to coincide with the premiere of the movie.
3 The design has been **patented** so nobody can copy it.
4 Our coffee is **produced** using the finest coffee beans from Kenya.
5 It is thought that the sandwich **was** invented in 1762.

14.2

A 4
B 1
C 7
D 8
E 2
F 5
G 3
H 6

14.3 🔊 Model Answers

1 Our accounts are audited every May by a separate department.
2 The coffee blends we produce are approved by our professional coffee tasters.
3 All passengers' luggage is scanned by security staff when they go through Departures.

4 All our marketing material for the Asia office is designed by Jane.
5 All the orders are checked by our packing department before delivery.
6 The database is updated with customers' details by Stephen.
7 All our ingredients are bought from Fair Trade suppliers by our cosmetics buyer.
8 New lines are added to our women's fashion range on a regular basis by Nicola.
9 The new product tracking app for customers was invented by Jason.
10 Our new website was launched by our marketing team in January.

14.4

1 False
2 False
3 True
4 Not given
5 True

14.5 🔊

1 These toys can't have been checked.
2 A discount should have been given.
3 The order can't have been taken by her.
4 A free bag can be given to every customer.
5 Faults in the products shouldn't be ignored.
6 Our prices can't be beaten.
7 His order must have been placed late.

14.6 🔊

1 Next, the ingredients **are mixed** together to make a cake mixture.
2 Then the cake mixture **is poured** into cake pans.
3 Next, the cakes **are put** in a hot oven.

④ When the cakes are cooked, they **are taken** out of the oven.

⑤ The cakes **are left** to cool on a wire cooling rack.

⑥ Finally, the cakes **are assembled** and decorated with icing.

15

15.1

OPINION:
fantastic, **amazing**, **excellent**

SIZE:
huge, **tiny**, **large**

AGE:
ancient, **modern**, **state-of-the-art**

COLOR:
magenta, **crimson**, **black**

NATIONALITY:
Indian, **Turkish**, **Chinese**

MATERIAL:
leather, **metal**, **plastic**

15.2 ◄))

① It's made by a fabulous, young Indian designer.

② I love these fantastic, small, blue china bowls.

③ We're launching an outstanding new range of clothes.

15.3 ◄))

① What a lovely **stylish** desk you have!

② Sam asked me to design a **classic** brown chair.

③ I brought back some delicious **Turkish** candy from my trip.

④ Do you like this **pretty** crimson watch for ladies?

⑤ Do you like our cute **green** teddy bear for our new children's range?

⑥ Our competitors are selling **unfashionable** black suits.

⑦ Our team is developing an innovative **leather** interior for our executive car.

⑧ I love buying large **yellow** flowers for the office.

⑨ Jane has bought an **expensive** classic car at an auction.

⑩ We have an amazing **Italian** coffee machine in our office.

⑪ I have ordered some of those fabulous **double-sided** business cards.

⑫ We have an amazing **grey** oven in our staff kitchen.

⑬ This is our new **lightweight** digital camera.

15.4

① B
② A
③ B
④ A
⑤ B

15.5

① False
② True
③ True
④ False
⑤ Not given

15.6 ◄))

① Their website is easy to use because it has a **simple**, effective style.

② Zander's Pizzeria makes **delicious**, oven-baked pizzas.

③ I love this **comfortable**, leather armchair.

④ The new, **full-color** brochure is very bright and attractive.

⑤ I like the **clean**, new rooms in that hotel.

⑥ Those small, **diamond** earrings are beautiful.

⑦ My dad drives a **huge**, black truck.

⑧ Ella makes high-quality, **cotton** curtains.

⑨ We aim to give **excellent** customer service.

⑩ We offer a **unique**, personal experience.

⑪ I don't like those ugly, **wooden** desks. They're hideous!

⑫ This modern, **Japanese** car is much faster than my old one.

⑬ What a **gorgeous**, big photo of all the team!

16

16.1 ◄))

① logo
② slogan / tagline
③ brand
④ radio advertising
⑤ billboard
⑥ poster
⑦ sponsor
⑧ door-to-door sales
⑨ copywriter
⑩ word of mouth
⑪ coupons
⑫ free sample
⑬ market research
⑭ consumer
⑮ promote
⑯ sales pitch
⑰ merchandise
⑱ social media
⑲ unique selling point / USP
⑳ television advertising
㉑ online survey
㉒ leaflet / flyer
㉓ advertising agency

17

17.1 🔊

EXTREME:
enormous, **terrible**, **brilliant**, **furious**, **fascinating**, **exhausted**, **awful**

ABSOLUTE:
true, **wrong**, **perfect**, **equal**, **impossible**, **unique**, **empty**

CLASSIFYING:
metal, **electronic**, **scientific**, **woolen**, **industrial**, **organic**, **rural**

17.2 🔊

1 The factory was totally destroyed.
2 I was thoroughly exhausted this morning.
3 The warehouse is almost empty.
4 Jon is an extremely good speaker.
5 Peter is fairly good at Spanish.
6 The project is largely complete.
7 Sian is an utterly brilliant swimmer.

17.3 🔊

1 **Fairly** certain. I think I sent it yesterday.
2 Yeah, it's absolutely **fantastic**. I love it.
3 It was very impressive, but **almost** identical to mine!
4 Yes, it's totally **unique**. I have the only one.
5 That's right. **Nearly** everyone likes him.
6 No. It was **absolutely** awful. I almost fell asleep.
7 It was practically **empty**. There were only a few people there.

17.4

1 absolutely fantastic.
2 utterly original.
3 almost impossible.
4 very busy.
5 extremely important.
6 completely new.
7 highly reflective.
8 practically impossible.
9 absolutely amazing.
10 really clever.
11 fairly certain.

18

18.1

1 B
2 A
3 A
4 B
5 A

18.2 🔊

1 There was **such** a large crowd outside.
2 The results were **so** disappointing.
3 We've had **such** a fantastic year.
4 The price for the hotel was **so** high.
5 The week seems to pass **so** slowly.

18.3 🔊

1 This coffee was so expensive.
2 My colleague is so lazy.
3 Clara's presentation was so interesting.
4 That is such a depressing book.
5 The sales were so disappointing.
6 It's such a strange story.
7 It's so important to be on time.

18.4

1 Not given
2 True
3 True
4 False
5 Not given

18.5 🔊

1 Our senior managers think the price of our products is **too** high.
2 This room won't be big **enough** for this afternoon's meeting.
3 The team is **so** excited about tonight's awards ceremony.
4 I thought today's meeting was **such** a waste of time.
5 Jim doesn't speak loudly **enough**. I can barely hear him.
6 Our IT system is **so** old. It's time we invested in a new one.
7 The new intern works **so** slowly. She prefers talking on the phone.
8 Our products were **too** expensive to appeal to middle-market customers.
9 Mary is **such** an ambitious woman. She wants to be a CEO by the age of 30.
10 You shouldn't drive **too** quickly when you're in this part of town.
11 The strikes have caused **such** a problem for our employees who commute.
12 The marketing campaign was **too** boring to appeal to young people.

19

19.1 🔊

1 You shouldn't work so hard.
2 You could do a training course.
3 You should get some fresh air.
4 You must give him a call.
5 You should order some more.

19.2 🔊
1 You **could** try delegating the task to your team. I'm sure they'd do a great job.
2 Greg **ought to** apologize to his team for his behavior. He was very rude.
3 Antonio really **ought to** employ some new staff, or we'll never meet our deadline.
4 We **should** organize a training course for the interns.
5 The secretary really **should** ask her boss for a raise. She works very hard.

19.3 🔊
1 You **should walk** to work if the train is canceled.
2 You **ought to call** the IT desk about your new password.
3 You **shouldn't eat** your lunch at your desk. Go to a café instead.
4 You **must tell** your manager when you want to book time off.
5 Clare **ought to take** a break if she's tired of her job.
6 You **could do** an English course if you want to learn English.
7 Dave **ought to go** home if he's not feeling well.
8 Pete **shouldn't talk** to the public about company secrets.

19.4
4

19.5 🔊
1 Why don't we **organize** a feedback session?
2 What about **asking** Pedro to do it?
3 Why don't you **hire** some new staff?
4 What about **buying** a new printer?
5 Why doesn't Mabel **go** on vacation?
6 Why **don't** they close the Mumbai branch?
7 What about **inviting** the clients to dinner?

19.6
1 Why don't we file these documents?
2 You should take a vacation for a week.
3 You shouldn't eat your lunch at your desk.
4 What about hiring a new member of staff?
5 Why don't you work from home on Fridays?

19.7 🔊
1. What about asking Pete to do it?
2. What about organizing a workshop?
3. What about selling our products online?
4. Why don't we ask Pete to do it?
5. Why don't we organize a workshop?
6. Why don't we sell our products online?

19.8 🔊
1 What about organizing a workshop?
2 Why don't we arrange a meeting?
3 What about buying a new printer?
4 Why don't we hire a new secretary?
5 What about asking Cyril to help?
6 What about providing free software?
7 Why don't we book a meeting room?

19.9 🔊
1 You ought to ask the clients for more time.
2 How about talking to your co-workers about your problems?
3 We could hire some new interns next year.
4 Why don't you quit your job if you don't like it?
5 You should complete the project before the deadline.

20

20.1 🔊
1 a bonus
2 an appraisal / a performance review
3 to approve
4 to delegate
5 performance
6 to be promoted

20.2 🔊
1 telephone manner
2 fast learner
3 IT / computing
4 data analysis
5 attention to detail
6 numeracy
7 written communication
8 problem-solving
9 time management
10 work well under pressure
11 able to drive
12 public speaking
13 teamwork
14 research
15 organization
16 leadership
17 decision-making

21.1 🔊

1 Tom **can** fix your car this afternoon. It will be ready at 5:00.
2 Karl **can't** drive. He failed his driving test again.
3 Jon used to be really nervous, but now he **can** give presentations.
4 She **can** type really quickly. She types over 60 words per minute.
5 I **can't** work the new photocopier. It's too difficult.
6 Hansa is a really good cook. She **can** cook really nice Indian food.
7 Ali **can't** read my handwriting. He says it's really messy.
8 Ania **can** speak French. She learned it in college.
9 Petra **can't** manage her staff any more. They do what they like.
10 Parvesh **can** write clear reports. They are easy to read.

21.2

1 Past
2 Present
3 Present
4 Past

21.3 🔊

1 Janice **can't** tell me if sales are up until she gets the final reports in.
2 Phil loves meeting new people, so he **can** work in the HR department.
3 Saira **couldn't** type fast, but now she can type 60 words a minute.
4 Ed **can** write reports very well. I'm going to ask him to help me write mine.
5 Keira **couldn't** use the database, but now she trains people in how to use it.

6 For years Alex **couldn't** speak Arabic, but now he has done a beginners' course.

21.4

1 False
2 False
3 Not given
4 False
5 True
6 True

21.5 🔊

1 He would do well in a smaller team.
2 She can manage her new team much better.
3 Before, he wouldn't talk in public.
4 She could train staff to do them.
5 She wouldn't be a good trainer.
6 He could be head of the department.

21.6 🔊

1 David has given his team excellent training. Now they can do anything.
2 Have you seen his brilliant designs? He can create our banners.
3 No one could read the boss's handwriting. It was terrible.
4 Sebastian is a very proactive person and would do well in marketing.

21.7 🔊

1 We think you are very talented and **would** be a great addition to our department.
2 I don't know what is wrong with the coffee machine. I **can't** get it working.
3 My confidence is much better now. Before, I **couldn't** give presentations.
4 Laila couldn't negotiate with her old boss, but she **can** with her new boss.

22.1 🔊

1 This training is really interesting. It is a lot of fun, **too**.
2 Team-building days are useful. They are **also** fun.
3 Some people always wash their coffee cups, **while** others don't.
4 **Although** Team A did the task quickly, Team B didn't finish it.
5 Team A built the bridge very quickly. Team B was **equally** successful.
6 Team A helped each other, **while** Team B disagreed with each other.
7 Hard work is an excellent trait in a team, **whereas** laziness is terrible.
8 Yesterday's training was useful. **However**, this morning's task was pointless.
9 Some people want to lead a team, **while** others are happy to be team members.
10 It is important to say what we all think. We should listen to each other **as well**.
11 This training is very useful. It is **equally** a good way to get to know people.

22.2 🔊

1 Although Sam went to the training day, he didn't learn anything new.
2 Team A solved the problem really quickly. Team B was equally successful.
3 This training is useful for managers. It is also useful for team members.
4 Some people want to be managers, while others want to be team members.
5 Laziness is a terrible trait for a team member, whereas honesty is excellent.
6 We'd like all staff to follow our usual dress code for the training. Please be on time, too.

22.3

- (A) 3
- (B) 1
- (C) 6
- (D) 5
- (E) 4
- (F) 2

22.4 🔊

1. The team-building task was useful and it was also a lot of fun.
2. Team A had to build a bridge, whereas Team B had to make a pizza. / Team B had to build a bridge, whereas Team A had to make a pizza.
3. While Team B completed the task first, they had some problems.
4. Training courses are really useful and they are often fun as well.
5. Team A worked together very well. Team B was equally cooperative. / Team B worked together very well. Team A was equally cooperative.
6. This task will identify your weaknesses, but also your strengths.
7. Our team baked a cake. However, the activity didn't matter.
8. Although the other team came first, we worked well together. / Although we came first, the other team worked well together.
9. Yesterday's task was easy, while today's task was more difficult.
10. Team A finished the task quickly, whereas Team B took its time. / Team B finished the task quickly, whereas Team A took its time.

22.5 🔊

1. As a consequence, I am now a team leader.
2. Consequently, they all won a medal.
3. For this reason, I was very nervous.
4. As a result, everyone attends them.
5. Consequently, she was promoted last week.

22.6 🔊

1. Team-building days are great for morale. **Consequently**, the atmosphere in our office is good.
2. We have regular IT training sessions. For this **reason**, everyone has good computer skills.
3. We do team building every year. As a **consequence**, we work really well together.
4. During team building we meet new staff. **For this** reason, we know our co-workers well.

23

23.1 🔊

1. We plan **to launch** our new product range at the conference.
2. Would you consider **organizing** the accommodation for the visitors?
3. I really enjoy **taking** clients out for dinner at famous restaurants.
4. Jenny has offered **to meet** our visitors at the airport.
5. I keep **suggesting** that we should have a staff training session.

23.2 🔊

1. Our clients expect **to** receive good customer service.
2. Would you consider **making** the name badges for the delegates?

3. Colin has offered **to organize** the training program for the new staff.
4. I hope **to impress** our clients when I show them around the new office.

23.3

1. Entertaining clients
2. To receive good customer service
3. They give their honest opinion
4. Their competitors had had one
5. Offer team-building events

23.4 🔊

1. I regret **to tell** you that I can't take the clients out for dinner. I'm very sorry.
2. Do you remember **calling** Dan last month? He has a question about a discount you offered.
3. Sue stopped **to read** the program for the launch event. It looked really interesting!
4. He regrets **telling** her his idea for the event because she copied it.
5. David gave his presentation, and went on **to talk** about new events.
6. I stopped **giving** my presentation because the CEO had a question.

23.5

- (A) 4
- (B) 1
- (C) 6
- (D) 8
- (E) 2
- (F) 7
- (G) 5
- (H) 3

23.6 🔊

1. I really enjoy entertaining new clients.
2. Sandra invited me to attend the overseas sales conference.
3. My manager asked me to book the accommodation.
4. Tom expects his manager to give him a promotion soon.
5. My boss asked me to give him an update on recent sales.
6. We invited all our customers to come to our party.

23.7 🔊

1. I enjoy entertaining our clients.
2. I remembered entertaining our clients.
3. I remembered to meet our clients.
4. I remembered to book accommodation.
5. She remembered entertaining our clients.
6. She remembered to meet our clients.
7. She remembered to book accommodation.
8. She enjoys entertaining our clients.
9. We enjoy entertaining our clients.
10. We remembered entertaining our clients.
11. We remembered to meet our clients.
12. We remembered to book accommodation.
13. They enjoy entertaining our clients.
14. They remembered entertaining our clients.
15. They remembered to meet our clients.
16. They remembered to book accommodation.

24

24.1 🔊

1. to take minutes
2. to look at
3. to take questions
4. to be absent
5. to reach a consensus
6. to run out of time
7. a strategy
8. main objective
9. action points
10. to give a presentation
11. to send out an agenda
12. to interrupt
13. attendees
14. to suggest / propose
15. unanimous agreement
16. to review the minutes
17. a show of hands

25

25.1 🔊

1. She said she could speak Thai and Mandarin.
2. She said she needed to talk to Hansa in HR.
3. He said he was working on the sales report.
4. He said he had finished the presentation.
5. He said he had been to the Mumbai office.

25.2 🔊

1. She **said (that) the taxi was outside**.
2. He **said (that) he needed to call the US office**.
3. He **said (that) he would get the bill**.
4. He **said (that) he couldn't open any emails**.
5. She **said (that) she had sent the order to them**.

25.3 🔊

1. She said she was busy that afternoon.
2. He said that he didn't like his new boss.
3. They said they hadn't received the delivery.
4. He said he was going to be in Tokyo that week.
5. They said they had been to the new product launch.
6. She said she would issue an invoice right away.
7. He said the company could give a 5 percent discount.
8. She said she had gotten along well with the interviewer.
9. They said they were designing a new range.

25.4

A 5
B 1
C 4
D 6
E 3
F 7
G 2

25.5 🔊

1. He **told** me that he'd been to China twice.
2. She **said** that she was going to Montreal.
3. He **promised** that he wouldn't be late for the train.
4. He **explained** that he didn't know how to use the photocopier.

5 He **denied** that he had broken the coffee machine.

6 She **complained** that the food was cold when the waiter brought it.

7 He **confirmed** that the tickets had been booked.

25.6 🔊

1 She **promised** to call me back after 2:30 that afternoon.

2 He **added** that he needed a copy of Simon's report about the year-end accounts.

3 She **explained** that the new all-in-one printer wasn't difficult to use.

4 He **confirmed** that he'd like to buy 100 units of the new product.

5 He **complained** that he wasn't happy with the customer service he had experienced.

6 She **suggested** that we should ask Ameera what she thought.

26

26.1 🔊

1 Selma asked me where you had put the annual report.

2 Krishnan wanted to know why I was late for work again.

3 My boss asked me what I thought about the new IT system.

4 Hans asked me where we would have the presentation this afternoon.

5 Sophie asked Claude why he wasn't at the meeting.

6 Tabitha asked me who had taken her cell phone.

7 Fiona wanted to know who had taken the minutes.

26.2

1 False
2 True
3 False
4 Not given
5 True
6 Not given
7 False
8 True
9 True

26.3 🔊

1 make a suggestion
2 get fired
3 make a mistake
4 do your best
5 do someone a favor
6 get a job
7 do research
8 make notes

26.4 🔊

1 She **asked me how many people worked in the company**.

2 He **asked me why I had handed in the report so late**.

3 He **asked me who had gotten / got promoted**.

4 He **asked me who the new senior manager was**.

5 He **asked me which candidate I had chosen**.

6 He **asked me how long I had worked here**.

7 She **asked me why I had been so late this / that morning**.

8 He **asked me what time I got home**.

9 He **asked me where I had had the appointment**.

10 She **asked me which printer I preferred**.

26.5 🔊

1 He **asked me if / whether the package had arrived safely**.

2 She **asked me if / whether I could do her a favor**.

3 He **asked me if / whether he could have a word with me later**.

4 She **asked me if / whether I had finished writing the report yet**.

5 He **asked me if / whether he could make a suggestion**.

6 She **asked me if / whether I had read last year's report**.

7 He **asked me if / whether I was coming to the awards ceremony on Saturday**.

8 She **asked me if / whether I had enjoyed the presentation**.

9 He **asked me if / whether I had booked a table at the restaurant**.

27

27.1

1 True
2 True
3 False
4 Not given
5 False
6 True
7 Not given
8 True
9 Not given
10 False

27.2 ◀))

1 Unfortunately, we have a few problems with our production line.
2 Regrettably, few people have the skills necessary to run a multinational company.
3 So few of our customer reviews are positive that it's becoming a problem.
4 I have little doubt that the conference will be a success.

27.3 ◀))

1 **Few** employees have worked for the company for as long as Sofia.
2 We have **a little** bit of time before the meeting ends.
3 So **few** companies offer this service that demand is sure to be high.
4 Very **little** can be done to improve facilities in the short term.
5 We can expect **a little** increase in profits over the summer season.
6 It's great that you have **a few** ideas about how we can improve sales.

27.4 ◀))

1 I'm sure all will be well once you've spoken to the customer.
2 All I know is that the order is late.
3 Is that all you need?
4 All we can do is wait for a response from the client.

27.5 ◀))

1 There are a few things we can do to improve staff morale.
2 We've had little interest in our new app.
3 Little can be done to improve staff morale.
4 So few people have money to spend on our luxury vacations.
5 Our new app is very popular.

28

28.1 ◀))

1 What is our target this year?
2 Who is handling the account?
3 Who is in charge?
4 What is your sales target?
5 Who responds to complaints?
6 Who spoke to Mr. Jones?
7 What is our plan of action?

28.2 ◀))

1 Do I need to dress formally?
2 Did you quote this price?
3 What should I tell the client?
4 Who wants to work in New York?

28.3 ◀))

1 We should increase our margins, **shouldn't we**?
2 I didn't send you the report, **did I**?
3 She'll be a great manager, **won't she**?
4 I'm not getting a raise, **am I**?
5 We haven't made a loss, **have we**?
6 We're going to win the award, **aren't we**?
7 Louis has worked here since 2012, **hasn't he**?
8 Brett worked late last night, **didn't he**?

28.4 ◀))

1 We could launch our product early, **couldn't we**?
2 Jakob ordered the samples, **didn't he**?
3 We can't cut prices any further, **can we**?
4 We haven't achieved our target, **have we**?
5 We need to improve product quality, **don't we**?

6 We're not ready for the meeting, **are we**?
7 They are opening a new store, **are they**?
8 You weren't in London last week, **were you**?
9 You traveled to Paris by train, **didn't you**?
10 I'm writing the proposal, **aren't I**?
11 I emailed the right person, **didn't I**?

28.5

1 Not given
2 True
3 False
4 False
5 False
6 True
7 False

28.6 ◀))

1 What was her name? I didn't **hear** it.
2 **Who** is responsible for training?
3 You're not worried about the meeting, **are you**?
4 **What** is our timetable for this project?
5 Sales are better than expected, **aren't they**?
6 Sorry, I **missed** that.

29

29.1 ◀))

1 tourism
2 finance
3 energy
4 mining
5 recycling
6 manufacturing
7 agriculture / farming
8 catering / food

9 hospitality
10 fashion
11 electronics
12 real estate (US) / property (UK)
13 chemical
14 entertainment
15 pharmaceutical
16 healthcare
17 fishing
18 transportation
19 education

29.2

1 organized
2 team player
3 practical
4 responsible
5 motivated
6 calm
7 confident
8 reliable
9 innovative
10 punctual
11 accurate
12 ambitious
13 professional
14 energetic
15 creative

30

30.1

1 I want to apply for **a** job in **an** office.
2 I've got **an** interview next week for **the** job I told you about.
3 **The** ideal candidate enjoys working in **a** team.
4 **The** deadline for applications for **the** job in IT is next Monday.
5 Please complete **the** form on **the** job page on our website.

30.2

A 8
B 1
C 7
D 5
E 3
F 6
G 2
H 4

30.3

1 Nurses often have to work very long hours. They are very important people.
2 Working hours are from 8:30 to 5:00. Lunch is from 1:00 to 2:00.
3 Vale loves giving training sessions. The training sessions she gave yesterday were amazing.
4 The job I applied for is based in Madrid. It's in sales and marketing.
5 The people who interviewed me for the job were really nice. They were managers.
6 I have just applied for a job in the finance department at your company.
7 The salary for this job is not very good. I don't think I'll apply for it.
8 The successful candidate will have three years' experience branding new products.
9 Our company is currently recruiting more staff for the Paris office.
10 I have meetings with the CEO and some of our new clients today.
11 Marisha is good at pitching products. It's the thing she enjoys most about her job.
12 This job requires in-depth knowledge of business trends in the wider world.

30.4

1 False
2 True
3 True
4 False
5 True

30.5

1 We need someone who is willing to travel, and can speak **Spanish**.
2 Tara works in **the finance department** of an advertising agency.
3 Marc and Samantha often travel to China **on business**.
4 The company is based in the UK, but it does business throughout **the EU**.
5 I started looking for a job as **an engineer** after I finished college.

31

31.1

1 I graduated from college in June 2016 with a degree in chemistry.
2 I am writing to apply for the role of head chef.
3 I heard about the job on your website.
4 I am fully trained in all aspects of health and safety.

31.2

1 Jim graduated **from** college with a degree in physics. Now he is a research scientist.
2 He is fully trained **in** all aspects of sales and marketing. I think he'll do a great job.
3 In my role as Senior Program Developer, I reported **to** the Director of IT.

④ Tanya has applied **for** a job in the marketing department of our company.
⑤ I worked **for** the owner of a leading hairdressing salon. I learned a lot from him.

31.3

Model Answers
① Ellie has worked in marketing for more than ten years.
② She developed award-winning campaigns in key markets.
③ She introduced a new customer-focused branding initiative.
④ She is responsible for training junior members of staff.
⑤ She looks after the Europe region.
⑥ She describes herself as energetic, dynamic, and extremely reliable.

31.4 ◀))
① skills
② salary
③ a position
④ to apply for a job
⑤ to report to someone
⑥ a team
⑦ a résumé
⑧ an opportunity
⑨ to amount to

31.5
Dear Mr. Chang,

I am writing to **apply for** the position of Senior Sales Consultant, as advertised on your website.

I have **worked in** the sales industry for more than eight years, and am **trained in** selling a range of products to varied markets. In my current position, I am **responsible for** sales to Asian markets, and last year I **looked after** the new market of China, where sales **amounted to** more than $10 million.

I am **passionate about** working in the sales industry and welcome the opportunity to learn new skills. I run the training program for new staff members and ten of the junior sales consultants **report to** me. In their training, I **focus on** developing awareness of the most effective sales strategies.

Please find my résumé and references attached. I look **forward to** hearing from you.

Yours sincerely,
Deepak Singh

32

32.1 ◀))
① The person **who** I admire the most in the company is the Sales Manager.
② The office **where** I work is a tall, modern building.
③ The customers **who** gave us feedback were all very positive.
④ The team **that** I lead is fully qualified and highly motivated.

32.2 ◀))
① We sell apps **that are designed by IT specialists**.
② We are based in an office **that is in the business park**.
③ I work with clients **who have high standards**.
④ This is the reason **that I applied for this job**.
⑤ Spain and Italy are the countries **where we sell the most**.

32.3 ◀))
① Training staff, **which** is my favorite part of the job, is really interesting.
② In my current job, **where** I serve lots of customers, I have learned to deal with complaints.
③ My boss, **who** is very understanding, encourages me to leave the office on time.
④ While I was in college I worked in a café, **which** taught me a lot about customer service.

32.4
Ⓐ 3
Ⓑ 5
Ⓒ 1
Ⓓ 6
Ⓔ 2
Ⓕ 4

32.5 ◀))
① Last summer, **when** I had just graduated, I worked as an intern in a bank.
② My teacher, **who** was an amazing person, inspired me to study law.
③ My apprenticeship, **which** I completed in 2016, was in IT.
④ The place **where** I want to work as a tour guide is New York.

32.6 ◀))

1 Tom's team, whose staff are hard-working, hit their sales targets last month.
2 In my previous job, which was in sales, I learned to give presentations.
3 I sometimes work from home as it is the place where I can concentrate best.
4 My clients, who expect good customer service, said my work was excellent.

32.7 ◀))

1 The thing **that gets** me excited is when we hit our sales targets.
2 People **who know** me well say I am customer-focused and give good customer service.
3 I have a can-do attitude, **which means** that I get things done.
4 I would hope to receive more than my current salary, **which is** $45,000 a year.
5 My boss, **who is** quite understanding, would allow me to leave after a month's notice.

33

33.1 ◀))

1 to touch base
2 a change of pace
3 a game plan
4 to be on the same page
5 up in the air
6 up and running
7 in a nutshell
8 to go the extra mile
9 to fill someone's shoes
10 groundbreaking
11 to clinch the deal
12 to call it a day
13 to cut corners

14 to be ahead of the game
15 a ballpark figure
16 to do something by the book
17 to corner the market

34

34.1 ◀))

1 Alex comes up **with** great ideas.
2 Hal looks down **on** his co-workers.
3 I'm **looking** forward to the launch.
4 Fred **puts** up with a lot of noise.
5 She comes **across** as rather superior.
6 The printer has run **out** of paper.
7 Jim's staff get **away** with being late.
8 Shona has to **face** up to poor sales.
9 We need to **keep** up with the schedule.

34.2 ◀))

1 I get along with my team.
2 She comes across as friendly.
3 I can't put up with his music!
4 He comes up with good ideas.
5 Tom gets away with a lot.
6 We have run out of coffee.
7 We must face up to facts.

34.3

Model Answers
1 Some companies think social media is trivial.
2 Social media helps you keep up with trends.
3 ABC Foods uses social media to tell customers news about the company.
4 ABC Foods has previews of its TV ads.
5 The company does this so that subscribers feel they are keeping up with company news.

6 Competitions make ABC Foods stand out from its competitors.
7 Customer loyalty means customers make repeat purchases.

34.4 ◀))

1 I'll look **them** up online.
2 Can you fill **it** in?
3 I'd like you to take **it** on.
4 I can't let **them** down.
5 Can we talk **it** over?
6 Could you look **it** over?
7 We are giving **them** away.
8 I need to call **it** off.
9 I can't figure **them** out.
10 The taxi will pick **him** up.
11 I keep putting **it** off.
12 Yola turned **it** down.

34.5

1 Update your website
2 To find new ideas for your product
3 Translating social media use into sales
4 Sharing users' questions and answers

34.6 ◀))

1 Cev always comes up with great ideas.
2 Dan and Sam don't get along with each other.
3 The copier has run out of paper.
4 Here's a form. Can you fill it in?
5 Rohit keeps up with the business news.

34.7 🔊

1 I looked **up** the candidates on social media. They all looked very talented.

2 Kennedy's team **gets away with** a lot. It's not fair on the others.

3 You're leading an important pitch today. Please don't **let me down**.

4 Can you take **on** writing the sales report today, or are you too busy?

5 We're giving **away** free books to customers. We hope it will increase sales.

35

35.1 🔊

1 She will get a raise in her new position.

2 You won't get a bonus.

3 We may ask him to become a mentor.

4 We might need to recruit more staff.

5 We may have to fire her.

35.2

1 True

2 True

3 False

4 False

5 True

35.3 🔊

1 Our staff can't use the new database. We might have to provide more training.

2 David has over 15 years' experience and he will lead our marketing department.

3 I need your report by Thursday. You might need to work overtime.

4 Anna's laptop is broken. She will get a new one this week.

5 There is a pay freeze at the moment, so you won't get a raise.

6 If Rita's work doesn't get better, we may have to fire her.

7 We have some meetings in France. You may have to go to Paris.

8 We can't hire any staff at the moment, so you might not get an assistant until March.

9 If your presentation goes well, the CEO might ask you to give it to the board.

10 Tanya has been promoted. She will lead a team next year.

11 Dev has had a bad trading year. He won't meet his sales targets.

12 Paula always goes the extra mile. She will make a great addition to the team.

35.4 🔊

1 He will definitely be promoted.

2 You will probably get a raise.

3 She probably won't need training.

4 They'll definitely get a bonus.

5 I probably won't go on vacation.

6 I definitely won't change jobs.

7 We will probably hire an intern.

8 He probably won't meet clients.

9 It will definitely sell well.

35.5 🔊

1 You will **probably** be promoted.

2 He will **definitely** get the job.

3 She **definitely** won't get a raise.

4 They will **probably** get a bonus.

5 I **probably** won't get a new laptop.

6 You will **definitely** get a company car.

7 I will **probably** move to the head office.

8 You **probably** won't need much training.

9 We will **definitely** hire a new assistant soon.

35.6 🔊

1 Katrina doesn't have much experience. She **will probably** need more training.

2 Meliz has to travel to see clients. She **will probably** get a company car.

3 Mr. Cox has complained about our service. He **probably won't** use us again.

4 The negotiations are going quite well. We **might** clinch the deal tomorrow.

5 You're doing a great job, but our profits are down. You **might not** get a raise.

35.7

Model Answers

1 Isaac met all his sales targets this year.

2 Isaac might be promoted next year.

3 Isaac will mentor two new employees from next month.

4 Isaac will start selling products in Asia.

5 Isaac might need additional training.

6 The company thinks Isaac will perform well.

36

36.1 🔊

1 microphone

2 USB drive / flash drive

3 voice recorder

4 cursor

5 low battery

6 power cable

7 touch screen

8 handout

9 speakers

10 computer

11 laminator

12 video camera
13 lectern
14 keyboard
15 printer
16 cue cards
17 mouse
18 laptop
19 webcam
20 pointer
21 router
22 chairs
23 projector

36.2 ◄))
1 report
2 flow chart
3 graph
4 pie chart

37

37.1 ◄))
1 Let's now turn to future prospects.
2 My talk today is about building brand loyalty.
3 Do feel free to tweet your questions to me.
4 So, we've looked at our market penetration.
5 To sum up, this year has been difficult.
6 We'll look at case studies, and then I'll take questions.
7 The purpose of this talk is to share sales figures.

37.2 ◄))
1 To **sum** up, it's been a very successful year for us.
2 We'll **look** at the competitor's products, then I'll introduce our new product.

3 Do **feel** free to interrupt if you'd like to comment.
4 So, we've **looked** at problems we need to overcome.
5 Now let's **turn** to the solutions to those problems.

37.3 ◄))
1 microphone
2 keyboard
3 USB / flash drive
4 cursor
5 handout
6 lectern
7 cord

37.4
1 Not given
2 False
3 Not given
4 Not given
5 True
6 True

37.5
A 4
B 3
C 7
D 5
E 1
F 2
G 6

38

38.1 ◄))
1 If we home in on our Barcelona store, we can see it is successful.
2 All regions achieved their sales targets, aside from the Southwest.

3 Customer response has been positive, excepting Eastern Europe.
4 Generally speaking, our products are popular in South America.
5 With the exception of February, sales are up.
6 This year the company is focusing on its social media campaign.
7 If we focus on this chart, we can see sales have dropped.

38.2 ◄))
1 Excepting East Asia, our sales **have grown by more than 10 percent**.
2 In actual fact, the consumer group said **they really liked our prototype**.
3 As a matter of fact, I don't think **Alyssa is suitable for the role**.
4 For instance, we've had a lot of positive **feedback about our menswear**.
5 In general, the number of subscribers **to our magazines is falling**.
6 Concentrating on the basics, there are **many areas where we can improve**.
7 Jorge needs to improve key skills such **as dealing with customers**.

38.3 ◄))
1 In **reality**, there is no way of knowing what sales will be like next year.
2 In **fact**, we need to hire about 10 more staff this year.
3 **However**, we can't really afford to hire more staff.
4 **Except** for Janice, all staff in this department deserve a raise.
5 **Actually**, there is little we can do to increase production.
6 **Generally**, staff seem very happy with working conditions.

38.4

1. False
2. Not given
3. True
4. Not given
5. Not given
6. True

38.5 ◀))

1. If we **home** in on profits, we can see growth.
2. If we focus **on** prices, it's clear they're too high.
3. **By** and large, our T-shirts are our bestseller.
4. In **reality**, there's no way we can recover.
5. As a **matter** of fact, I am very disappointed.
6. Except **for** Korea, I've been to most of Asia.
7. **In** general, China is our biggest market.

39

39.1 ◀))

1. This sports car is **the fastest** car on sale today.
2. Our leather jackets are **more fashionable** than our competitors' jackets.
3. This digital camera is **the best** model ever.
4. Our new microwave oven is more efficient **than** any other model.
5. This ice cream maker is **easier** to use than any other on the market.
6. Our customers said our sofa is **more comfortable** than other models.
7. Our organic vegetables are **fresher** than supermarket vegetables.

8. Book a train trip with us in advance to get **the cheapest** fares.
9. Our cake range was voted **the tastiest** on the market in a recent survey.
10. These batteries last **longer** than the leading brand.
11. We think our new winter coat is **the warmest** on the market.

39.2

1. the biggest
2. cheaper
3. more energy-efficient
4. more stylish

39.3 ◀))

1. We will create **the most beautiful** flowers for the tables and the bride's bouquet.
2. Our drink is **healthier** than that brand because it has a natural caffeine substitute.
3. Our fitness tracker is **just as effective as** more expensive models, but is cheaper.
4. We offer **better technical support than** other cell phone companies do.

39.4 ◀))

1. This pizza is as tasty as the leading brand, but much cheaper.
2. Our budget clothing is as stylish as other brands on the market.
3. These store-brand dishwasher tablets are as good as the market leader.
4. Our latest action movie is as exciting as anything you've ever seen.
5. This eco-friendly dishwashing liquid is not as good as the leading brand.

39.5

1. as exciting as
2. more simple / simpler
3. more convenient
4. the healthiest
5. the best
6. just as cheap as / cheaper than

40

40.1

Ⓐ 3
Ⓑ 1
Ⓒ 4
Ⓓ 2
Ⓔ 8
Ⓕ 5
Ⓖ 6
Ⓗ 7

40.2 ◀))

1. There has been an increase in complaints.
2. There was a dramatic spike last year.
3. The price is fluctuating wildly.
4. We expect a considerable drop in prices.
5. There was a sharp rise in the share value.
6. The share value has rallied slightly.

40.3 🔊
1 Staff numbers went **from** 120 to 150.
2 **Between** 15 and 18 percent of stock is unsold.
3 We've experienced a boom **of** 56 percent.
4 Profits have fallen **by** 11 percent.
5 The share price peaked **at** $22.
6 Complaints doubled **in** the last quarter.
7 Our sale was **between** May and June.

40.4
1 Not given
2 True
3 False
4 Not given
5 False
6 True

40.5 🔊
1 There's been a **dramatic spike** because of a poor harvest.
2 Our sales **peaked at** $200,000 a day in December.
3 Yes, malfunctions have **fallen steadily** since last year.
4 Between **20 and 30** percent of our stock is on sale.
5 Yes, they've **rallied slightly** since last year.
6 There was an **increase of** 10 percent in the cost of electricity.

41.1 🔊
1 Are you able to pay **our fee in installments**?
2 We might move forward with the contract **if you would consider buying in bulk**.
3 I would like to resolve this issue **as soon as possible**.
4 Maybe we could discuss some **alternative options for the design**.
5 We were thinking **that you could design our new logo**.
6 I'm afraid I was hoping for **something more innovative**.

41.2
Ⓐ 3
Ⓑ 4
Ⓒ 1
Ⓓ 6
Ⓔ 2
Ⓕ 5

41.3 🔊
1 I was wondering where I can try these clothes on.
2 Could you tell me when the sample designs will be ready?
3 I was wondering if I could talk to you about Samia's performance.
4 Could you tell me whether I can order this product in store?
5 I was wondering whether you have paid my invoice yet.
6 Could you tell me what the warranty period is?
7 I was wondering how the new product is different from the old one.
8 Could you tell me when the price list will be available?

9 I was wondering if you would be able to offer me a discount.

41.4 🔊
1 I'm afraid **our deadline was missed**.
2 It looks as if **the wrong size was sent**.
3 It seems that **the discount was not applied**.
4 I'm afraid **our order was delivered** to the wrong address.
5 It looks as if **the price was calculated** incorrectly.
6 It seems that **your employees are not very well trained**.
7 I'm afraid **our customers were not satisfied**.
8 It seems that **my order was lost** while it was being delivered.
9 I'm afraid **my steak was not cooked** properly.
10 It looks as if **a mistake has been made**.
11 It seems that **the printer still hasn't been fixed**.
12 I'm afraid **the document was not checked** thoroughly enough.

41.5 🔊
1 I was wondering if **you could** look at my presentation.
2 Could you **tell** me when my order will be dispatched?
3 I was wondering if you **would** be free to meet tomorrow.
4 Could you tell me when **we can** expect our invoice to be paid?
5 I was wondering what time **the store opens**.
6 Could you **tell me** how much the new product should retail for?

41.6
2

42.1 ◄))

1 If you ask me, you won't find a better deal.

2 Actually, we are waiting for the factory to send us more of that product.

3 The main thing is that we agree on schedule dates.

4 What I'm saying is that I can offer free delivery on orders over a hundred.

42.2

1 True
2 True
3 False
4 Not given
5 False

42.3 ◄))

1 **Actually**, we sent you an email with them this morning.

2 I'm afraid not. If **you ask me**, this is a great deal.

3 What **we need is** an assurance that you can meet our schedule dates.

4 The **main thing is** that we agree on a price that allows enough profit.

5 **I'm afraid** your asking price is too high. Can we say $40 a unit?

43.1 ◄)) Note: All answers can also use the contracted form of "would."

1 If they **gave** us a discount, we **would place** an order.

2 If the product **was** cheaper, we **would buy** it.

3 If they **moved** the deadline, we **would meet** it.

4 I **would reply** to the email now if I **had** more time.

5 We **would sell** more online if our website **was** faster.

6 We **would send** the package tomorrow if you **ordered** before 9 tonight.

7 If the agency **sent** us better temps, we **would use** them again.

8 If I **worked** late every night, I **would finish** my report for Friday.

9 I **would apply** for the job if the hours **weren't** so long.

43.2

1 True
2 Not given
3 False
4 False
5 True
6 False

43.3 ◄))

1 If customers don't pay on time, we charge a 15 percent late fee.

2 Our helpline is open from 8am to 8pm if you need help.

3 When employees work weekends, they get paid double time.

4 If you are a regular customer, we give you a 5 percent discount.

5 If we receive a payment after 3pm, we credit it the next day.

43.4 ◄))

1 If you need help with your computer, **you can call the IT department**.

2 We would move production to Europe **if it was cheaper to do that**.

3 We will issue a full refund **if you return the product to one of our stores**.

4 If clients are regular customers, **we give them a 5 percent discount**.

5 If our receptionist was rude to you, **we would give her a verbal warning**.

43.5 ◄))

1 If you **don't / do not** pay on time, we won't send you your order.

2 We'll issue a full refund if **you're not / you are not** happy with our products.

3 If you **book** two nights in our hotel, we'll give you a third night for free.

4 If Alan's presentation **goes** well, he will get promoted next month.

5 We won't charge you for your stay if you **don't / do not** get a good night's sleep.

6 If you **order** over 100 units, we'll give you a discount.

43.6 ◄))

1 Well, if you pay for the overtime, **we will finish** the job by then.

2 Yes. If **clients buy** 100 units or more, we give them a 5 percent discount.

3 If you return it to us within 28 days, **we will issue** a full refund.

4 If **you could do** a price of $59 per unit, we'd sell it in our stores.

5 We're sorry to hear that. If a customer makes a complaint, **we take** it very seriously.

6 We can't do that yet. If **we took** on more staff, we'd be able to increase production.

44.1 🔊

Note: All answers can also use contracted positive forms and long negative forms.

1. We **would have signed** the contract if the deadline **hadn't been** so tight.
2. If we **had left** earlier, we **wouldn't have missed** the train.
3. If the waitress **hadn't been** so rude, we **wouldn't have** complained.
4. If we **had ordered** before 3pm, we **would have received** the goods today.
5. We **wouldn't have lost** the client if we **had delivered** the report on time.
6. If you **had repaired** the printer, we **wouldn't have canceled** the contract.
7. If I **had known** how expensive it was, I **would have put** it in the safe.
8. The boss **wouldn't have shouted** if you **had admitted** your mistake.
9. If you **had been** more prepared, you **would have given** a better presentation.
10. We **would have given** you free delivery if you **had paid** on time.
11. If I **had known** our competitor's price, I **would have offered** a bigger discount.
12. We **would have met** our deadline if we **had employed** more staff.
13. If you **hadn't been** off sick, we **would have invited** you to the meeting.
14. We **would have paid** the full amount due if you **hadn't missed** our deadline.
15. If you **had sold** more products last time, we **would have asked** you to lead the pitch.

44.2
1. B
2. A
3. B
4. A
5. B

44.3 🔊
1. If I'd used the spell check, **my work wouldn't have had so many errors**.
2. If she'd told the boss about her mistake, **he wouldn't have been so angry**.
3. If they'd paid on time, **we wouldn't have canceled their order**.
4. If I'd used the latest sales data, **my report would have been up to date**.
5. If he'd checked the order was right, **his clients wouldn't have complained**.
6. If you'd ordered more units, **we would have given you a discount**.
7. If he'd wanted an older model, **he would have asked for one**.

44.4 🔊
1. Clive will get a verbal warning **unless his timekeeping improves**.
2. **Unless you pay** by the end of today, we will cancel the contract.
3. We won't win the contract **unless we can** offer a better price.
4. I won't get promoted this year **unless I impress** the boss.
5. Your warranty will not be valid **unless you register** your product.
6. **Unless I sell** to 100 new customers, I won't meet my sales targets.
7. We won't make many sales **unless we beat** our competitors' prices.
8. **Unless I work** overtime, I'm not going to meet the deadline.
9. His presentation will be boring **unless he adds** special effects.
10. The CEO won't be happy **unless we win** the contract.
11. **Unless you lower** the price, we won't order any more units.
12. We will miss the train **unless we leave** now.

44.5
1. True
2. False
3. Not given
4. True
5. True

44.6 🔊
1. We would have hit our sales target if the internet **hadn't gone** down.
2. If he **had left** earlier, he wouldn't have been late for the meeting.
3. If you had been less rude, we **would have won** the contract.
4. The CEO would have promoted me if she **had seen** my presentation.
5. If we **had lowered** the price, we would have made more sales.

Acknowledgments

The publisher would like to thank:
Amy Child, Dominic Clifford, Devika Khosla, and Priyansha Tuli for design assistance; Dominic Clifford and Hansa Babra for additional illustrations; Sam Atkinson, Vineetha Mokkil, Antara Moitra, Margaret Parrish, Nisha Shaw, and Rohan Sinha for editorial assistance; Elizabeth Wise for indexing; Jo Kent for additional text; Scarlett O'Hara, Georgina Palffy, and Helen Ridge for proofreading; Christine Stroyan for project management; ID Audio for audio recording and production; David Almond, Gillian Reid, and Jacqueline Street-Elkayam for production assistance.